The Tea Ceremony

Sen'ō Tanaka

The Tea Ceremony

SEN'Ō TANAKA
SENDŌ TANAKA

Preface by Edwin O. Reischauer
Foreword by Yasushi Inoue

KODANSHA INTERNATIONAL
Tokyo • New York • London

PHOTO CREDITS
Motoki Seiichi, page 125. Tabata Minao, pages 17, 112, 121–23, 127. The
Gotoh Museum, pages 61–71. Tokue Akihiko, front jacket, back jacket,
pages 22–24. Additional photographs supplied by Dai Nihon Chadō
Gakkai.

Permission to reproduce photographic material was graciously granted
by the following: Imperial Household Agency (the stepping stones of
Katsura Imperial Villa on page 112, right); Myōki-an (the stepping stones
of Tai-an on page 112, left); The Gotoh Museum (the tea utensils on pages
61–71); Yamanashi Prefectual Library (the illustration on page 181).

NOTE: With the exception of the author credits, Japanese names appear
in the traditional Japanese order, surname preceding given name.

Distributed in the United States by Kodansha America, LLC, and in the
United Kingdom and continental Europe by Kodansha Europe Ltd.

Published by Kodansha International Ltd., 17–14 Otowa 1-chome,
Bunkyo-ku, Tokyo 112–8652.

First cloth edition, 1973
First paperback edition, 1982
Revised edition, 1998
Revised paperback edition, 2000
20 19 18 17 16 15 14 13 12 11 10 09   15 14 13 12 11 10 9 8 7 6

www.kodansha-intl.com

CONTENTS

P R E F A C E

For the foreigner, it is hard to bring Japan into clear focus. Is the real Japan to be found in mammoth tankers, soaring production figures, and seething mobs of commuters, or does it still reside in cherry blossoms, geisha, and Mt. Fuji? Is it the fleeting glimpse from the window of the "bullet train" of a thatched cottage in a neatly tailored, verdant valley surrounded by gently bending bamboo, or is it the train itself—that epitome of late–twentieth-century technology and social engineering? Is it the fanatic soldiers of the Imperial Army of a generation ago or the equally determined young Japanese of today, locked in desperate combat with a brutal examination system, or circling the globe with earnest intent to discover the whole world and imbibe its essence? Is it the serenity of medieval gardens and Buddhist sculpture or the pollution and traffic jams of Tokyo and Osaka? Is it the inner calm of Zen philosophy or the red tape and frustrations of modern urban life? Japan is, of course, none of these, but it is all of them and a great deal more.

It is unreasonable to think that all the rich diversity of Japan can be brought into a single sharp focus. How could we do this for our own countries? I cringe when I hear Japanese attempting to interpret the vast complexities of the United States by some single touchstone—be it the Puritan spirit, Thoreau, Lincoln, the frontier spirit, capitalism, Vietnam, or whatever. The rich culture of the British Isles cannot be reduced to one single equation, much less that of Japan, which today and throughout recorded history has had at least twice the population of the British Isles.

Still, some aspects of a civilization do stand out as being especially revealing of the best in that culture. They hint at, even if they do not fully define, those underlying strata of the psyche that give a culture its flavor and distinctiveness. The tea ceremony is certainly one of these features for Japan. It cannot bring all of Japanese civilization into focus, but it does offer a window that looks deeply into the Japanese soul.

Unfortunately, the tea ceremony is not a window that is easily opened. It has often proved as mystifying to foreigners as informative.

In a nation that loves tradition, the tea ceremony over the centuries has become so heavily encrusted with the barnacles of tradition that it has all but lost forward motion as a means of artistic expression. Transformed in modern mass society into a polite accomplishment for all girls of breeding, it has become a homogenized mass product. Enshrined as part of the mystique of a unique Japanese culture, it is casually sampled, along with seaweed or raw fish, by hordes of twittering foreigners. I can remember seeing rows of disinterested tourists gulping down their allotted tea before rushing on to the next "experience," while loudspeakers blared forth about the spirituality of the tea ceremony. I can remember one particularly grotesque episode, when a couple of dozen news photographers smashed down the surrounding sliding doors in their eagerness to take flashbulb shots of Mr. and Mrs. Robert Kennedy accompanied by my wife and me, attempting to look as though we were enjoying a quiet aesthetic moment.

Despite all this mistreatment, however, the tea ceremony does run deep and strong and pure. I am no specialist on the subject, but I have had enough intimate experience with it to be sure that this statement is true. In my days as a graduate student in Kyoto, my wife took flower arrangement lessons from a lady teacher who also taught the tea ceremony. Over a period of several months, I joined her once a week at her teacher's home to participate in tea ceremony sessions. Neither of us studied how to make or serve the tea, but we did learn how to play our role as participants in what became increasingly a deeply felt aesthetic and spiritual experience. In a sense we moved into a different world in time and space. There was no schedule. Everything moved at a slow pace quite detached from the rest of our lives. Our attention focused down to just a few objects of beauty, again quite removed from the world of overflowing abundance outside. There was a sense of sinking deep within one's own self, of being at harmony with nature, of finding all in very little.

I find it hard to describe the experience, but I know that it has given me an understanding of aspects of Japanese culture that I otherwise would never have had. There really is something very important to be seen through the window of the tea ceremony, if one can but brush aside the encrustations of long tradition and the flimflam of tourism and mass society. Many Japanese have attempted to help us peer through this window. *The Book of Tea* of the great art critic and thinker, Okakura Kakuzō (usually called Tenshin by the Japanese), was the first important effort more than two generations ago. Now Sen'ō Tanaka, a leading authority on the tea ceremony, offers his masterful guidance in this magnificent book. The tea ceremony is no "open sesame" for all of Japanese civilization, but it does offer a way to learn something about the innermost qualities of the Japanese and the riches they have to offer the world.

EDWIN O. REISCHAUER

F O R E W O R D

It would perhaps be superfluous to repeat once again what an important role *chadō* played in the molding and shaping of Japanese culture. The tea ceremony, together with its basic aesthetic concepts of *wabi* and *sabi*, is one of the traditional arts of which we today are proud inheritors. *Chadō* has influenced our outlook on life, it has colored our beliefs and attitudes as well as the standards that so rigidly govern the Japanese people. Even the youth of today, although they may have no interest in the tea ceremony, find it difficult to detach themselves from these strong traditional values that will remain with them all their lives.

Just as "Rome was not built in a day," the tea ceremony, too, was not developed in a short space of time. Its roots and origins are intricately interwoven with the historical development of Japan, and in order to understand the deeper, more spiritual aspects of its philosophy, it is imperative to refer to its long history, starting with the introduction of tea to Japan, the changes in the custom of tea-drinking during the Heian and Kamakura periods, and culminating in the lives of the great masters of tea who advanced the art. Men like Shukō and Jōō were the first to adopt Japanese terms and expressions in the art of the tea ceremony, and Rikyū, the most famous of them, with his disciples Sōtan, Oribe, Enshū, Sekishū, and Fumai, did much to illuminate the dark avenues of culture in their time.

It is almost impossible for one to write about the tea ceremony without complete immersion in the mainstream of Japanese cultural history. Furthermore, it is difficult, even for a Japanese, to relate the art of the tea ceremony, which constitutes so much philosophic thought, without meandering from the spiritual stream of its concept; yet, Sen'ō Tanaka has succeeded admirably.

He has concentrated all his efforts on preserving what is most valuable in *chadō*, and as president of the Dai Nihon Chadō Gakkai and a young master of the tea ceremony in Japan, he has done much to promote its popularity in this country. It has always been my belief that a history of *chadō* can only be written by a master who has dedicated his whole life to the tea ceremony. This book could not have been produced had Mr. Tanaka been only a scholar of the art, for it requires more than an academic treatise to conjure up, in everyday language, the spirit that lies within the walls of the tea room.

When the custom of drinking tea was first introduced to Japan, it was only too natural for its devotees to want to design a special room for this purpose. I say only too natural here, but there is no other country in the world, apart from Japan, where such tea rooms exist, and, therefore, this expression is really only applicable to the Japanese people. Thus, the foundation of *chadō* was laid when the first tea room came into existence, and its essence was present within this room even though it took centuries for the art to evolve into its present form.

With the establishment of tea rooms, special rules of etiquette that suited the atmosphere were inevitably created, and special utensils that preserved and enhanced this decorum were selected by tea masters who dedicated their whole lives to perfecting the ceremony. Thus, the tea room served as a salon where men could come to enjoy peace of mind and purity of spirit, and at the same time appreciate art at a very refined and sophisticated level. The tea room also became a refuge where the hustle and bustle of daily life could be forgotten, replaced by a discipline of mind and body.

Yet what is truly amazing is that nothing special or extraordinary takes place. The host and guests simply engage in the act of making and drinking tea. But it is this act that is important, for in the smallness of the tea room, the whole universe—heaven, earth, and life itself—can be evoked, or, as in the case of Rikyū, death confronted.

Mr. Tanaka is one of the very few tea masters born in the Shōwa period, and by writing this book he has added another leaf to the pages of the tea ceremony. He follows the path of the earlier great masters of tea who wrote of the ceremony in their lifetime. This, I believe, is the responsibility of all great tea masters throughout history.

This book, written with the Westerner in mind, follows *The Book of Tea* by Okakura Kakuzō (Tenshin), who published his classic in English in 1906. It is my heartfelt desire that this volume will, as Tenshin's did, enhance an understanding of Japanese culture. And, in conclusion, I would like to wish Mr. Tanaka great success in his noble pursuit.

YASUSHI INOUE

PREFACE TO THE NEW EDITION

It is nearly a quarter of a century since Sen'ō Tanaka first wrote *The Tea Ceremony*. The Dai Nihon Chadō Gakkai (Japan Association of the Tea Ceremony), which was founded in 1898, is now approaching its centennial. In 1990, moreover, the establishment of the Santoku-an Foundation, named after a famous tea house, made possible the inauguration of the Tea Culture Prize (Chadō Bunka Gakujutsu Shō) and promotional subsidies, as well as activities aimed at spreading the culture of tea overseas. Due in part to Japan's great economic strides, the past twenty-five years have also seen a tremendous surge in international awareness of Japan. All in all, the time seemed ripe for a new edition of this book, and so I undertook the task of revising my father's work.

When he first began writing this book, my father was opposed to using the word "ceremony" in the title. He yielded, however, after the editors urged him to produce a book that would convey the essence of Japanese tea culture and resolve any misleading impression that may have been created by the popularly accepted term "tea ceremony." Given that it is exceedingly rare for a single phrase to span two cultures and completely convey the nuances of tradition across linguistic barriers, it probably does little good to haggle over individual words. Of paramount importance is the essence that lies behind the phrase. As I carried out the work of editing and revising my father's book, I tried to remain true to that spirit.

Concerning the content of the book, the organization of the chapters has been altered, and many passages have been rewritten to make them even more accessible to readers desiring to learn about the tea ceremony. The purpose—to convey the essential spirit and meaning of the ceremony—is virtually unchanged, but explanations relying on outdated factual information underwent thorough revision. The opening pieces Mr. Reischauer and Mr. Inoue graciously consented to write for the original edition are as appropriate today as they were during the lifetimes of these two distinguished gentlemen, and have been retained.

Photographs in the current edition are all new. The previous selection was made with an eye to introducing foreign readers not only to the tea ceremony but to the Japanese scenery and seasonal changes that influenced it. Today, many more readers will have visited Japan in person, and numerous excellent books of photographs dealing with Japanese scenery and life are available. Accordingly, more pages have been given over to photographs that illuminate the spirit and techniques of the tea ceremony itself.

It may seem odd for a mere reviser to have his name listed as co-author. The initial resistance I felt to the suggestion grew out of my understanding of the exclusive nature of copyright. Yet historically, a tradition is passed along by many people carrying out unauthorized revisions of their predecessors' work—by people making every effort to adapt teachings to their own age, without damaging the teachings' essence. In the long run, we are all revisers of tradition, waiting to be followed in turn by the next generation of revisers. In Japan, this process has been termed *michi*, or "way." Using another reading for the same ideograph (*dō*), the idea of a "way" finds expression in such words as *chadō*, the way of tea; *kadō*, the way of flowers; *kōdō*, the way of fragrance; and *kendō*, the way of the sword. Understanding of the tea ceremony and of Japanese culture can, I believe, be greatly enhanced by focusing on the nature of this continuity of past and future which has played such a crucial role in building traditional Japanese culture.

The result of revision may be decline or decay, preservation of the status quo, or a sudden leap forward. Time, rather than the revisionist himself, decides which it will be. All the reviser can do is accept the result of what he has done as a judgment on his grasp of the essence of things, and on his assessment of his own time.

The many people who assisted me in producing this book join with me, I am sure, in the hope that it may find favor among even more readers than before.

SENDŌ TANAKA

INTRODUCTION

*C*hanoyu, which literally means "hot water for tea," is known in English as the tea ceremony and has as its objective a relaxed communion between the host and his guests. It is based in part on the etiquette of serving tea, but it also includes the aesthetic contemplation of landscape gardens, tea utensils, paintings, flower arrangement, and all the other elements that coexist in a harmonious relationship with the ceremony. Its ultimate aim is the attainment of a deep spiritual satisfaction through the drinking of tea and through silent contemplation.

It is a unique composite form of art, created through the refinement of the Chinese custom of drinking tea, and distilled with elements of Zen philosophy, which gave it various symbols and rituals. On a different level, the tea ceremony is simply an entertainment where the guests are invited to drink tea in a pleasant and relaxing room. The bonds of friendship between the host and guests are strengthened in the ceremony when the host himself makes and serves the tea.

Each tea ceremony is supposed to be a unique experience, with its own particular mood that can never be duplicated. An expression was coined by the well-known master of the fifteenth century, Takeno Jōō, who performed each tea ceremony reverently because he believed it was "the one chance in one's lifetime." His famous pupil, Rikyū, took the lesson to heart when he shaved off all his hair for one of his master's ceremonies, as a mark of respect for the occasion.

The tea ceremony borrowed much from Zen religion because the first tea masters were priests, who, since the fourteenth century, had exerted a marked influence on Japanese culture and social customs. They taught their followers that enlightenment can only be reached through Zen meditation, and the tea ceremony became a means of disciplining the mind. Thus the saying "tea and Zen are inseparable" was born.

In the sixteenth century, when the art was handed down to the general population, the tea ceremony enjoyed widespread favor. Everyone, from nobles to commoners, found in it the ideal means of relaxation from the cares of the outside world; the tea room was a place where they could mix freely with anyone and yet cultivate their sense of appreciation of the forms of beauty in the setting and the use of special tea articles.

At the same time the spiritual aspect of the ceremony gave way, regrettably, to formal etiquette, as a special code of ethics was devised to govern the education of its devotees. This affected the general character of the tea cult, whose finer principles of inward spirituality were sublimated by an increased concentration on outward form.

There was a time when the tea ceremony was thought of as one of the accomplishments required of every well-brought-up young lady as a prerequisite of marriage. This was no doubt the result of a misconception that the study of tea was equivalent to the study of formal etiquette. While it is true that throughout its long history Japan has found many ways of associating with tea, for the purposes of this book I believe it most appropriate to concentrate on the spiritual tradition of the tea ceremony as encompassed in the word *chadō*, the Way of Tea.

Chanoyu is a specialist form of art that calls for a good knowledge of architecture, landscape gardens, and tea utensils, as well as the capacity to appreciate the total effect of their beauty. Thus it seems that etiquette, spirituality, *and* knowledge are all necessary elements for the understanding of the tea ceremony. In the large tea gatherings of today, it is difficult to convey all these refined qualities, for the art of the tea ceremony is, by its very essence, founded on intimacy, spontaneity, and subtlety.

SEN'Ō TANAKA

The alcove in the Santoku-an tea hut in Tokyo decorated for winter. The calligraphy is a verse about a mountain ascetic, Ling-shih Ju-chih, of the Yuan Dynasty. The simple bamboo vase was made by Sen no Rikyū. It contains a white camellia with a sprig from a small tree (*Stachrurus praecox*).

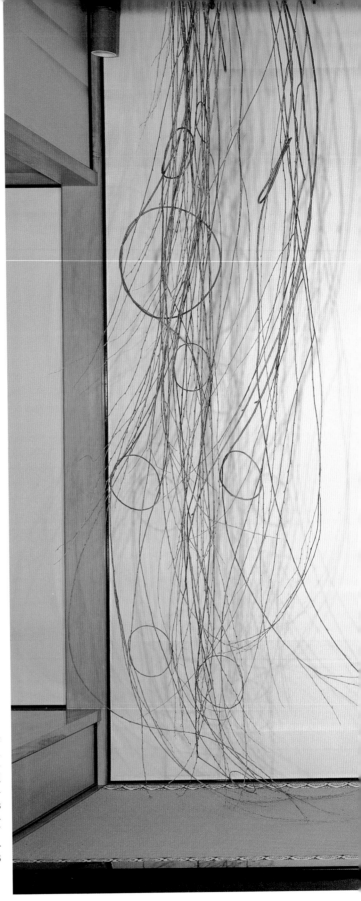

Willow branches and other symbols of longevity decorate the alcove for the New Year. Offerings on the red lacquered tray include lobster (the back bent like an old man is a popular symbol of long life) and a *daidai* citrus, whose homonym means "generations and generations," a wish for the prosperity of succeeding generations. The bronze vase contains light pink camellia and white plum. The calligraphy is a rendition of "Welcome the Spring," a common New Year's greeting, and was written by Emperor Reigen, who ruled from 1663 to 1687.

The setting for thick tea in October in the Santoku-an tea hut of Dai Nihon Chadō Gakkai, Tokyo. The brazier is placed in the center of the tatami, closer to the guests than usual, in anticipation of the arrival of winter and the change to the fire pit.

Thin tea setting using the fire pit in a *hiroma*-style room. The blue-and-white water jar by Eiraku (1795–1854) has a pine, bamboo, and plum design. The lacquered frame around the fire pit is decorated with chrysanthemum and paulownia crests. The *natsume* tea container has a chrysanthemum design. The tea bowl is *korai*-type from Korea.

Ladling hot water into the tea bowl.

Whisking the tea.

Finished tea.

The host placing a bowl of thick tea on the tatami, ready for the guest to take.

I

HISTORY

JAPANESE HISTORICAL PERIODS

PREHISTORIC
Jōmon ca. 10,000 B.C.–ca. B.C. 300
Yayoi ca. 300 B.C.–ca. A.D. 300
Kofun ca. 300–710
  Asuka 592–710

ANCIENT
Nara 710–94
Heian 794–1192

MIDDLE AGES (MEDIEVAL)
Kamakura 1192–1333
Northern and Southern Dynasties 1333–92
Muromachi 1392–1573
  Warring States 1482–1573

PREMODERN
Azuchi-Momoyama 1573–1603
Edo 1603–1868

EARLY MODERN / MODERN
Meiji 1868–1912
Taishō 1912–26
Shōwa 1926–89
Heisei 1989 to present

Early History of Tea

Reliance on China

Tea did not grow in Japan until the first seeds were brought from China during the T'ang dynasty (618–907), when cultural interchange between the two countries reached a peak. The first mention of a formal ceremony involving the drinking of tea is found in the eighth century, when Emperor Shōmu (reign, 724–49) is reported to have invited the monks who had participated in one of his religious services to take tea in his palace.[1]

At about the same time in China (760), a Buddhist priest by the name of Lu Wu completed the first book on tea called *Cha Ching*, which outlined all the rules for the correct method of making tea, such as the temperature of the hot water and the proper use of tea vessels. It was largely through the influence of this classic that the form and style of today's tea ceremony evolved in Japan.

During the Nara period (710–94) tea plants were grown in the grounds of some temples in Japan and tea served priests and noblemen as a medicinal beverage. As tea was not imported in large quantities from China and was not grown extensively in Japan, it came to be regarded as a luxury commodity beyond the reach of the general populace. Its general appeal was further restricted when relations between the two countries deteriorated toward the end of the T'ang dynasty, and the evolution of tea from medicine to beverage in China was not transmitted to Japan until much later on. At the same time, Japan, which had been imitating the more sophisticated culture of China, was now forced to mold its own traditions and foster its own culture.

One outcome of this new development can be seen in the way in which Buddhism in Japan took a different approach from Chinese Buddhism and crystallized into a purely Japanese religion. Similarly, the Japanese nobility began to create new pastimes built around aesthetic appreciation in the fields of art and calligraphy. As no records were kept of the Chinese custom of tea-drinking, the beverage remained virtually unknown from the Nara period until the Heian period (794–1192), but tea was reintroduced in different parts of Japan toward the end of the latter period and at the beginning of the Kamakura period (1192–1333).

It is almost certain that if tea had been native to Japan, or had been more readily available, the Japanese tea ceremony might not have been created, since its rules and formalities are based on the concept of tea as a rare and valuable commodity.

Introduction of Powdered Tea to Japan

The Kamakura period in Japanese history coincided to a large extent with the Southern Sung dynasty (1126–1279) of China, an epoch characterized by a high level of culture both in the fine and applied arts. A new systematic approach to studying philosophy and religion attracted a number of Japanese priests and scholars to travel to China. One of these priests, who left for China in 1187, was Myōan Eisai, the founder of Zen Buddhism in Japan. He returned to Japan in 1191 and some say planted the tea seeds he had brought with him in the Hizen district, later transplanting them to Hakata, Kyushu, where the first temple of his Rinzai sect[2] was built.

Eisai, it is said, was the first to grow tea for a religious purpose; others before him had cultivated tea for medicinal use only. It was at this time that tea was becoming associated with the newly formulated canons of Zen, and the word *sarei*, meaning the etiquette of tea-making, was often applied in a religious connection.

Whether Eisai actually grew any tea bushes himself is now a matter of debate. But there is no doubt that Eisai brought the custom of making tea from powdered leaves to Japan and was instrumental in spreading the idea. Prior to Eisai, people had steeped tea leaves in hot water. Eisai taught them how to grind leaves into a fine powder and mix it thoroughly with hot water.

Powdered tea was first mentioned in a book by Cai Xiang, a noted

Chinese calligrapher who worked under the Sung emperor Jen Tsung (1023–64). His book called *Ch'a Lu*, written in 1053, referred to the manufacture of powdered tea, the forerunner of the green tea that was incorporated into the tea ceremony in Japan. Another Sung emperor, Hui Tsung, referred to the bamboo whisk used to whisk the tea after water was poured over it in his book *Ta Kuan Ch'a Lun*, or *A General View of Tea*. These were the first two imports from China that formed the basis of the tea ceremony as we know it in Japan today.

Eisai aroused a great deal of hostility among the monks who disliked the new religious ideas he had imported, but he succeeded in enlisting the protection of the Kamakura shogunate, whose members were among his earliest converts. In January 1211 he wrote the first treatise on tea in Japan, *Kissa Yōjōki*, or *Tea-Drinking Is Good for the Health*, a small booklet of twenty pages in praise of tea. In his short treatise, Eisai strongly recommended tea as a cure for five types of disease: loss of appetite, paralysis, boils, beriberi, and sickness from tainted water. Tea, he added, is a remedy for all disorders, and this was perhaps the main reason for the consequent popularity of tea-drinking.

The priests were also among the first to appreciate tea as a beverage, especially Myōe of the Kōzan-ji temple in Toganoo. Myōe was said to have been given some tea seeds by Eisai, and the cultivation of tea became a part of Myōe's religious life. He produced excellent crops from those first seeds in Fukase, and it is said that the tea produced there today originates from the plantations of Myōe.

By the thirteenth century, tea was being cultivated in the Uji district, and tea plantations spread to various parts of Japan to meet the growing demand for tea. The number of tea drinkers increased rapidly, especially among the upstart samurai. This warrior class, which was beginning to seek a legal basis of government to counteract the aristocratic regime in Kyoto, turned eagerly to everything offered by the Sung dynasty: legal and political systems, religion, and, naturally, tea. It is quite probable that, had the court nobles still been in power, there would have been little opportunity for the import of new knowledge from outside Japan.

Tea and the Samurai

After the fall of the Kamakura shogunate in 1333, Japan was thrown into a state of confusion by the rivalries between the Northern and Southern dynasties. During the civil wars a new class of people came into existence—*gekokujō*, or the parvenus, whose extravagant lifestyle quickly attracted the attention of the public. Most of these upstart nobles were interested in tea-drinking for entertainment, and they often held large gatherings with their friends to enjoy tea and play *tōcha*,[3] a game that originated in the Sung dynasty of China.

The guests were tested on their ability to distinguish between *honcha* (literally "genuine tea"), a designation for tea grown at Toganoo, and other tea. Later, however, as tea came to be grown in many places around the country, the game developed into a test of the players' knowledge of tea regions, plantations, and names of specific kinds of tea. Betting soon accompanied these games, and the winners were presented with valuable ornaments, furniture, and even imported Chinese artifacts as prizes, which added to the excitement of the games.

Tōcha was played by people from all classes and was not confined to the nobility. There are frequent allusions to the games in the diaries of priests and nobles, and the *Taiheiki*,[4] a famous chronicle of a civil war, refers to one host of a *tōcha* gathering who offered one hundred different kinds of stakes, while another piled up one hundred rolls of dyed silk before the players, and a third provided ten different kimono as prizes. It seems *tōcha* was a way for the hosts to flaunt their wealth as well as an excuse for decorating their homes with precious works of art. Such art displays also added to the enjoyment of the game for the guests.

The system of serving tea was extremely elaborate. There were originally ten cups of four different kinds of tea for each guest, but soon the number of cups increased to twenty, thirty, fifty, and seventy, until it reached one hundred cups per person. A tea party in which fifty or sixty cups of tea were served in a ceremonial manner took a long time, so a banquet including the serving of liquor was held, and tea was drunk between courses. It was not unusual for such a party to last from early morning until far into the night.

It is unknown what procedures were followed in the drinking of the tea, but most probably cups were passed from one guest to the next. If there were a great number of people present it would have been impossible to serve tea in individual cups: for instance in a gathering of sixty-three people, if each guest drank fifty cups, it would have required 3,150 cups to entertain all of them. The technique of passing around one cup seems to have originated in these huge feasts, and probably explains why only one bowl is used in today's tea ceremony.

Another activity in which one object was shared among many participants was ceremonial incense-smelling, a popular recreation among court nobles. In this type of game the participants sampled four different kinds of incense, ten times each. The average number of guests was usually ten, and they would pass one incense burner among them. If more than one incense burner was used, the smell could vary according to the level of heat in the different burners.

This habit of sharing might seem odd today, but it stems from the samurai class, which had strong family ties, and when they gathered on important occasions it was the custom for the lord to take the first sip of saké from a large cup and pass it among his retainers as a reaffirmation of their close bonds.

Tea and the Ashikaga Family

Soon after the commencement of the civil war, Ashikaga Takauji (reign, 1338–58) became the first shogun of the Northern court. The Tenryū-ji temple at Saga, near Kyoto, was built by him in 1339 to commemorate the death of Emperor Godaigo, who had perished in the struggle between the Northern and Southern dynasties.[5] The chief priest at Tenryū-ji was a certain Musō Soseki (1275–1351), a leading Zen teacher and master of landscape gardening and architecture. This appointment opened the way for other Zen priests to play a more important role in worldly society, and the ensuing close harmonious relationship between religion and government had a profound influence on the tranquil and simple spirit that typified the Muromachi period.

During the rule of Ashikaga Takauji, the tea game was so popular that he had to issue a ban against it. At the same time, a new style of tea gathering was evolving, called *cha-e*, an older form of *chanoyu*, the formal tea ceremony of today. Nevertheless it was *tōcha* that enjoyed greater popularity among soldiers and common people, who also started to place small bets on tea guessing. The *Tōji Temple Chronicle* in Kyoto relates that in 1403 a shop in front of the temple was selling tea by the cup, an indication of the popularity of tea with the general public. Even priests and temple attendants of Kyoto indulged in the tea game. Another temple chronicle, *Kyōkaku Shiyōshū*, mentions a more ribald form of sport called the *rinkan* tea gathering, where taking a hot bath was combined with the pleasures of drinking tea.

In 1397 the third Ashikaga shogun, Yoshimitsu (reign, 1368–94), built an elaborate palace at Kitayama, Kyoto, where he used to entertain his friends. The palace design combined elements of both Northern and Southern Sung styles, and was called *karayō*, literally "Chinese style."

In the *Correspondence on Tea-Drinking* (*Kissa Ōrai*), which was written during Yoshimitsu's time, the order and ritual of a tea party were described in some detail. The guests, after enjoying the host's hospitality, left their banquet seats and went out to the garden, where there was an arbor for tea entertainment. The arbor was actually designed for moon-viewing, and a platform commanding a view in all directions was built on the roof of the pavilion. Hanging on the walls of the moon-viewing

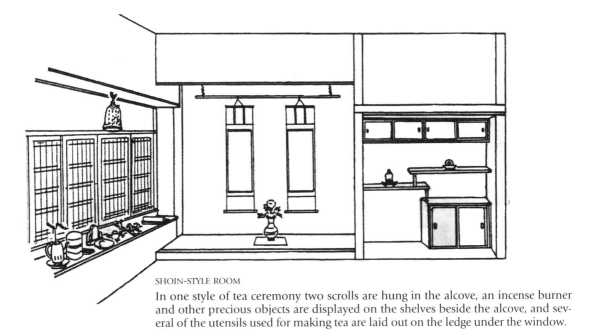

SHOIN-STYLE ROOM
In one style of tea ceremony two scrolls are hung in the alcove, an incense burner and other precious objects are displayed on the shelves beside the alcove, and several of the utensils used for making tea are laid out on the ledge under the window.

room were Chinese paintings and scrolls, and the guests relaxed with ten bowls each of four different kinds of tea.

It was the custom in those days to decorate homes and moon-viewing arbors with Chinese art, since the Kamakura culture was strongly under the influence of the Sung and Yuan dynasties. The priests who traveled between China and Japan frequently brought back important works of art with them, which they later displayed in their temples. The influence was to spread even further during the Muromachi period (1392–1573), when trade was intensified between Japan and Ming-dynasty China. In a record of the Enkaku-ji temple of Kamakura written in 1363 (*Butsu-nichian Kōbutsu Mokuroku*), there is a list of its Chinese possessions, which included twenty paintings by the famous Zen painters Mu-chi[6] and Yujian. In addition, the Ashikaga shogun's *Lists of Treasures and Paintings* (*Kundaikan Sōchōki*) also mention a great number of Chinese art objects that formed part of Japanese collections.

Japanese architecture of the Muromachi period was transformed from the formal palace style of the Heian period to a simplified samurai style, and then into the *shoin* style, which incorporated elements of temple architecture. *Shoin* details were adopted for the design of tea ceremony rooms: the alcove (*tokonoma*), for instance, developed from the decorative platform set in front of the Buddhist scroll in a noble's bedchamber, the pair of shelves (*chigaidana*) in the side of the alcove was formerly used to display precious ornaments, while the side alcove (*tsuke-shoin*) had a desk. The floor of these rooms was covered with tatami mats, in the *shoin* style.

Originally, the *shoin* room served as a study/drawing room, where visitors could also be entertained with tea. Near the drawing room was a shelf called *chanoyudana*, equipped with the necessary tea articles such as a charcoal brazier and a kettle, which enabled the host to make tea and carry it easily to his guests. The *chanoyudana* had also formerly been a part of temple design, and in the Muromachi period was incorporated into the interior of houses.

Gradually, the way of decorating the alcove, the shelves in the side alcove, and the *shoin* desk became fixed, with the aim of arranging a small number of articles aesthetically and functionally. This became a hobby of the samurai nobles, but was still inaccessible to the general public.

After some time, tea came to be served ceremonially in the *shoin* by menservants attired as monks, who were known as *dōbōshū*. The articles used for tea during this period were all imported from China: charcoal brazier, water jar, ladle stand, and lid rest. All these were arranged on a large utensil stand (*daisu*), and the ceremony was performed by the *dōbōshū*.

A fine example of *shoin* architecture may be found in the Ginkaku-ji (Silver Pavilion), which Ashikaga Yoshimasa (1435–90) constructed as part of his villa in Higashiyama, Kyoto, in 1482. The Silver Pavilion, in contrast to the Kinkaku-ji (Golden Pavilion), is more sophisticated in appearance, with an atmosphere that conveys a sense of profundity in its simplicity.

The Founder of *Chanoyu*

The tea ceremony vogue among the aristocrats attracted the attention of other classes as well, who sought to imitate the etiquette of tea-making developed by the samurai nobles, even though they could not afford the same magnificent rooms and decorations. This did not deter them from holding similar gatherings in smaller, less lavish rooms that were appropriate to their social status.

The samurai also used smaller rooms when they entertained only a few guests, since a small room was not only more comfortable but also

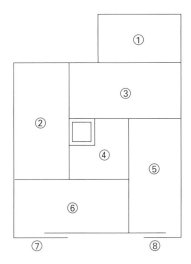

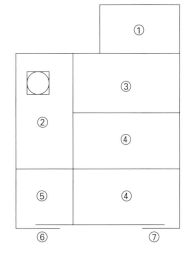

TEA ROOM WITH FIRE PIT

Layout of the tea room in the colder months when the fire pit (*ro*) is in use.

1. Alcove (*toko*). 2. Host's mat (*temae-datami*). 3. Distinguished guests' mat (*kinin-datami*). 4. Mat containing the fire pit (*ro-datami*). 5. Guests' mat (*kyaku-datami*). 6. Entry mat (*fumikomi-datami*). 7. Host's entrance (*sadōguchi*). 8. Guests' entrance (*nijiriguchi*).

TEA ROOM WITH BRAZIER

Layout of tea room in the warmer months when the fire pit is covered up and a portable brazier is used instead.

1. Alcove (*toko*). 2. Host's mat (*temae-datami*). 3. Distinguished guests' mat (*kinin-datami*). 4. Guests' mats (*kyakudatami*). 5. Entry mat (*fumikomi-datami*). 6. Host's entrance (*sadōguchi*). 7. Guests' entrance (*nijiriguchi*).

less formal. These small rooms were actually the corners of large rooms partitioned off by a screen, or *kakoi*, and later on, when smaller rooms were built specially for this purpose, they themselves became known as *kakoi*.

One of the best designers of smaller tea rooms was a Zen priest by the name of Murata Shukō (1422–1502), known as the father of the tea ceremony, for the spirit and etiquette of tea were originated by him. His actual existence had been called into question, but new data has since been found that throws some light on his life.

Shukō was born in Nara and entered the priesthood at Shōmyō-ji temple at the age of eleven. When he was twenty he left the temple, only to return again ten years later to enter the priesthood. He practiced Zen meditation under the monk and teacher Ikkyū Sōjun at Daitoku-ji temple in Kyoto. Shortly after he began his studies, he distinguished himself with his understanding of Zen, and was presented with a diploma signed by the Chinese monk Yuanwu. It is said that he hung the scroll of writing on the wall of his tea room in Nara and spent the rest of his days perfecting the tea ceremony as well as giving lessons to those who were interested in learning the art. From writings on Shukō, we can gain an insight into how passionately he tried to instill in his students the true spirit of simple, Zen-inspired tea.

Shukō initiated one important procedure that differed from those of earlier tea masters: he would serve tea to his guests himself. Although it was more usual to hold large tea gatherings in a *shoin* room, Shukō preferred the intimate and personal atmosphere of a small room where five or six people could communicate through the medium of tea. This became a fundamental ruling for all future tea ceremonies. The four-and-a-half-mat tea room (9 square yards/7.3 square meters) that he devised in order to create a more tranquil atmosphere for the performance of the ceremony had its origins in the Zen philosophy that Shukō had studied at Kyoto. He particularly disliked the undignified, boisterous *rinkan* tea gatherings of Nara, where the enjoyment of tea was combined with the ritual of a bath.

In a letter to his favorite pupil, Harima no Furuichi, Shukō outlined his own basic concept of the art of *chanoyu* and his personal outlook on aesthetics. He discussed the idea of refined simplicity, or *kareru*, at length, a theme that was much debated in his time, and he frowned upon the use of sophisticated, sober-colored pottery from Bizen and Shigaraki[7] by novices who had inadequate understanding of their aesthetic qualities. His letter also reveals that he took great pains to study the most aesthetic method of combining Japanese with Chinese tea utensils.

In the *Record of Yamanoue Sōji*, Shukō is referred to as *kaisan*, or the founder of the tea ceremony, an indication that Shukō was already highly regarded in his time by other tea masters. By contrast, Nōami,[8] the teacher of the shogun Ashikaga Yoshimasa, was only called a *dōbōshū*, and remembered as the one who had established the rules of ceremonial tea-making in the *shoin* tea room. Mention is also made of Shukō's preference for the four-and-a-half-mat tea room.

The language followed the new spirit of the age, and a host of new words were coined that combined the practical details of life with aesthetics: *suki*, for instance, meaning a "liking of tea," came also to mean "artistic taste." It was only in the sixteenth century that the expression *chanoyu* was used to describe a tea gathering where the host himself served tea for a small party of friends.

When the tea culture reached the peak of its popularity toward the end of the Muromachi period, tea devotees were given different titles to distinguish their relation to the art. *Chanoyusha* was the name given to a professional teacher of the tea ceremony like Shukō. A *wabi-suki* was a teacher distinguished by three particular qualities: faith in the performance of tea, an ability to act with decorum befitting a proper master, and excellent practical skills. Finally, the *meijin* not only met all the qualifications of the *wabi-suki*, but was a collector of fine Chinese tea utensils as well.

1. In the eighth century the Buddhist service included an event called *incha*, in which the emperor invited all the monks participating in the religious service to drink tea in the palace. It would seem that the custom of tea-drinking was adopted by the imperial family soon after it was introduced to Japan.

2. The Rinzai sect of Zen Buddhism is named after the Chinese monk Linji. In 1191, after four years in China, Eisai brought home the Rinzai faith, which he spread first in Chikuzen, then in Kyoto and Kamakura. Eisai's branch has now been divided into fourteen secondary branches, which possess over 6,400 temples and close to 1,200,000 followers.

3. While this tea-guessing game emerged in China in the eleventh century, historians are unsure of when or how the game found its way to Japan, where the game became popular in the latter half of the Kamakura period. Friends assembled to drink and enjoy tea as well as to test their skills in distinguishing different teas. Interest in *tōcha* persisted until the middle of the Muromachi period, and many lavish prizes were donated to the winners. In later days, the game became more refined, and came to be included in one variation of *temae* in the tea ceremony today.

4. The famous war chronicle in forty volumes that describes the battles between Japan's Northern and Southern dynasties from 1333 to 1392 is attributed to a priest called Kojima.

5. The two branches of the imperial family, which split into the Northern and Southern dynasties in 1333, fought for control of the country in a civil war that lasted fifty years.

6. A Zen monk and painter who lived during the late thirteenth century and is most famous for his "Eight Views of the Xiao Xiang Region."

7. Bizen pottery produced in what is now Okayama Prefecture is a fine-textured, red-bodied stoneware, originally produced for domestic use, but when tea masters turned to these wares after the fifteenth century the kilns began to produce numerous tea utensils. Old Bizen is usually unglazed, except for occasional accidental spots or smears of gloss. Shigaraki ware was produced from the Kamakura period in Shiga Prefecture and, compared to Bizen ware, is thicker in texture.

8. Nōami (1397–1471) was a painter and poet who served the Ashikaga household as the *dōbōshū* in charge of the evaluation of Chinese art. He is thought to be the author of *Kundaikan Sōchōki*, a catalog of works then in the possession of the Ashikaga family that is invaluable today as a source of knowledge of the art of the day.

Tea Masters and Tea Styles

The Beginning of the Modern Age

The sixteenth century proved an exciting age for Japan with the influx of Portuguese traders in 1550, who not only brought with them a new religion but also opened up new avenues of trade. This economic development brought about an expansion of the middle class, since the wealthy merchants who had profited by trading with the Europeans gained a certain amount of respectability, hitherto only reserved for the nobility. A delight in novelty and a spirit of adventure also characterized their ruler, a former daimyo, Oda Nobunaga (1534–82).[1] He opposed the traditional authority of the court nobles and wrested power from their hands during the civil wars, which were to last until 1600. Nobunaga governed the country along more democratic lines than did his predecessors, and this spirit of democracy was to have a strong impact on the ritual of tea.

Japanese architecture also developed along more inventive and more independent lines during his rule. While the Asuka period (592–710) had imitated Sui and T'ang styles, and the Kamakura period had depended on the Sung dynasty for new ideas, architecture during Nobunaga's time concentrated on distinctly Japanese designs in the construction of castles, homes, and tea houses. At the same time there was also a break in the older tradition of imitating temple designs in the construction of houses.

Perhaps it was a sign of the troubled times that the samurai warriors, acutely aware of the shadow of death following them from one war to the next, sought refuge from the grimness of life in the tea room. There, secure from the cares of the world, they were able to retreat peacefully into a spiritual universe. Perhaps too, for the same reason, they preferred to build and decorate their castles in a more flamboyant and colorful style than their predecessors. They did not hesitate to incorporate European designs in their homes, from architecture to furniture to clothes, and all of this was subsequently copied by the merchants.

The Tea Ceremony Is Introduced to Sakai

Today the city of Sakai is one of several small towns in the commercial and industrial complex of Osaka Prefecture, but in the two hundred years of the Muromachi and Azuchi-Momoyama periods, Sakai developed from a small fishing village into a prosperous commercial port. Trade with China was reestablished in the fifteenth century, with Sakai as the entrepôt between the two countries, and with the steady influx of merchants who came to trade in Sakai, it quickly became the most active business center in Japan.

The inhabitants of Sakai benefited financially under these conditions since the city was not ruled by feudal lords but was directly under the control of the city government. Its inhabitants were people of all classes, including priests, court nobles, and warriors. Residents of Sakai were usually referred to as *machi-shū*,[2] or those living in a self-governing town.

The administration of the city was carried out in fairly democratic terms by the *egō-shū*, or townsmen who met to formulate new laws. These men took pains not to tread on the toes of the powerful lords, and many meetings were convened to promote friendly ties with them. So, when the tea ceremony spread to Sakai, it rapidly became the most popular form of entertainment, since it made socializing so much easier than the complicated *renga* competitions where people gathered to compose strings of verse.

In early times, these tea gatherings were held in private homes, and anyone, whether he was acquainted with the host or not, could attend. It was rather like attending a gathering to admire works of art or eat a meal—anyone could casually join a group of people, regardless of his social status. This continued until more elaborate and rigid rules were devised, which excluded certain classes of people from mixing freely with their social superiors.

There were two leaders of the tea cult in Sakai: Torii Insetsu, who did not have much effect in his time, and Takeno Jōō, who distinguished himself in his lifetime by enriching the forms and accessories of the art. Both men were students of Shukō, the earlier master, and Jōō was well versed in poetry as well as in Zen Buddhism. He decided to enter the priesthood after fighting in the religious war of Yamashina, during which he had become acutely aware of the uncertainty of human life in the temporal world.

According to the *Record of Yamanoue Sōji*, Jōō had first practiced the tea ceremony according to the teachings of Shukō, but later on he improved on his master's techniques. Jōō's status as the leading master and innovator of his time was also enhanced by his large collection of over sixty kinds of tea utensils, when most of his contemporaries could only boast a few. Jōō's influence as a tea connoisseur even spread to Kyoto, where devotees copied his style of tea rooms, his arrangement of tea articles, his method of preparing tea, and his form of ceremony.

In the historical accounts given of the end of the sixteenth century, there is evidence that the advances the inhabitants of Sakai were making in the tea ceremony were more profound and refined than those in the other major cities. The samurai nobles, for instance, were still serving elaborate banquet meals to accompany their tea ceremonies, while the *machi-shū* entertained their guests on a much simpler level. This did not mean that they were less wealthy, but the philosophy behind their concept of the tea ceremony and its purpose differed greatly from the more vulgar ostentatiousness of the samurai. This ideal of simplicity in the art of tea was emphasized by Jōō in his teachings to his pupils. His outlook was expressed in a poem by Fujiwara no Teika:[3]

> Where are the crimson leaves,
> Flowers of the season?
> Only a little hut on the long curving bay
> Stands in the serenity of an autumn evening.

This, for Jōō, expressed the very heart and essence of the tea ceremony.

Toyotomi Hideyoshi and the Tea Ceremony

During the troubled age of Oda Nobunaga, the tea ceremony also came to be used as a means of courting powerful men. Nobunaga himself made use of the ceremony to impress the wealthy merchants of Sakai, who controlled the import of military weapons from Portugal.[4] For this purpose he invited the *machi-shū* to tea gatherings where he used tea utensils belonging to the Ashikaga clan, a diplomatic way of revealing that the authority of the Ashikagas was now vested in him. Frequently, he would make gifts of these articles as rewards to his generals. The articles were highly prized because of their association with distinguished previous owners. Thus the tea ceremony became popular even among the hardened military men of those times.

The successor to Nobunaga, Toyotomi Hideyoshi,[5] was well known for his political genius, and his rise from a lowly foot soldier to the ruler of the country. When he heard of Nobunaga's death, he rushed back from the front and disposed of Nobunaga's chief rival, Akechi Mitsuhide,[6] in a fierce battle[7] that ensued as part of the struggle for power. After Hideyoshi assumed complete control of the country, he often used the tea ceremony as a backdrop for political overtures.

Hideyoshi held a large tea gathering a month after he defeated Mitsuhide in 1582, and two more in the six months that followed. The third one, to which the leading merchants of Kyoto and Sakai were invited, took place in Yamazaki. Like Nobunaga before him, who made great show of using utensils that had belonged to his predecessors to flaunt his power, Hideyoshi would display Nobunaga's collection whenever he entertained his generals. In the same way, he wished to indicate that he was the rightful successor to Nobunaga through the use of his tea articles, which had once belonged to the powerful Ashikaga clan. Hideyoshi also acquired the habit of publicly exhibiting the collection of articles he had inherited. One such exhibition took place in 1583 after construction of Osaka Castle was begun.

Hideyoshi was appointed regent in 1585. As a token of his gratitude to the emperor and princes, Hideyoshi himself served tea at a small tea house inside the Imperial Palace. This was the first time that a ceremony was performed at court by a daimyo. Hideyoshi was so fond of the tea ceremony that he had a golden tea pavilion built the same year that could be carried with him to Kyushu.[8]

In 1587 a Great Tea Ceremony was held at Kitano, Kyoto. In announcing the occasion, Hideyoshi invited tea-lovers of all social classes to attend, but anyone failing to appear, he noted, would be barred from the tea ceremony thereafter. The statement indicates Hideyoshi's intent to dominate the tea world, and the fact that tea had already gained a wide following.

One interesting question that comes to mind is whether Hideyoshi used the tea ceremony only as a means of furthering his political career or out of a genuine interest in it. It is quite obvious that he entertained his political allies lavishly to display the valuable acquisitions he had inherited, but it is also true to say that he gradually found intense enjoyment in the art of *chanoyu* itself. It is written by chroniclers that Hideyoshi liked to meditate in a small hut when he was not entertaining on a grand scale.

In January 1584, Hideyoshi held a tea gathering in a secluded tea room of Osaka Castle. The ceremony itself was to commemorate the opening of this tea room, which was specially built for him. The room itself was only two tatami mats, or four square yards (about three square meters), and Hideyoshi often used it for intimate meetings with friends. A similar tea room was also built into Fushimi Castle, which Hideyoshi constructed after he handed the title of regent over to his son Hidetsugu. There, Hideyoshi spent his last years in complete tranquility and seclusion, showing a side of his character that was doubtlessly influenced by his teacher and master, Sen no Rikyū.

Rulers and Tea Masters

The relationship between rulers and tea masters existed since Nobunaga's time, under whom Hideyoshi was a general. When the inhabitants of Sakai refused to share the burden of Nobunaga's war expenditures, the tea master Imai Sokyū acted on Nobunaga's behalf to prevent a rebellion in Sakai. Tsuda Sogyū, head of the rich merchant class, cooperated with Sokyū, and his action earned him the friendship of Nobunaga, who often invited the merchant and tea master to his castles in Gifu and Azuchi. Sen no Rikyū was also a associated with Nobunaga. These three chief tea masters became the first *sadō*.[9]

Nobunaga held a tea gathering at Shōkoku-ji temple in Kyoto in 1574 at which merchants from Sakai were also present. At this ceremony he displayed a prized incense burner that he had named *chidori* (plover), and presented two of his *sadō*, Sōgyū and Rikyū, with the sacred *ranjatai* incense.[10] This gift to Sōgyū and Rikyū was an indication that he valued their friendship. Only Sōkyū, who was already held in great esteem by his ruler, was not presented with incense.

After Nobunaga's death at Honnō-ji temple, the three tea masters were forced to take sides to follow one or the other of the contenders for his title, Mitsuhide or Hideyoshi. Both Sōkyū and Sōgyū sent messengers to the two rivals inquiring after their health, but Rikyū lost no time in rushing to Hideyoshi's side.

After his victory, Hideyoshi retained all three of Nobunaga's tea masters, largely through necessity, in order to consolidate his power and make use of their connections. According to the *Record of Yamanoue Sōji*, Hideyoshi had eight masters working for him, although his biography reveals that he employed Sōkyū, Sōgyū, and Rikyū because of their close association with Nobunaga. Of the three, Rikyū came into greatest favor with Hideyoshi, a success which later generations were to attribute to the spiritual depth of Rikyū's ceremony. The historical accuracy of that interpretation of events is open to question. However, knowing how Rikyū's

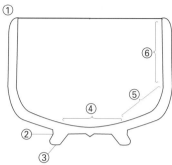
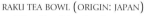

RAKU TEA BOWL (ORIGIN: JAPAN)
1. Rim (*kuchi-zukuri*). 2. Foot (*kōdai*). 3. Base of the foot (*tatami-tsuki*, lit. "place where the foot touches the tatami"). 4. "Tea-pool," indent at the bottom of the bowl where the remains of tea accumulate after drinking (*cha-damari*). 5. Whisking zone (*chasen zuri*). 6. Wiping zone (*chakin zuri*).

IDO TEA BOWL (ORIGIN: KOREA)
1. Rim (*kuchi-zukuri*). 2. Lower body (*koshi*). 3. Whisking zone (*chasen-zuri*). 4. Tea pool (*cha-damari*). 5. Cap (*tokin*, the small cap that mountain ascetics wear). 6. Foot (*kōdai*), in this case, a "bamboo joint" foot (*take-no-fushi kōdai*). 7. Wheel mark (*rokuro-me*). 8. Main body (*dō*).

image has been enshrined by tea devotees is an important key to understanding the practice of *chanoyu*.

Rikyū had been a pupil of Takeno Jōō, and his art was based on *wabi*, or the aesthetic of quiet elegance. While he was in Sakai he learned the "*daisu*" style of the ceremony, which was used in large *shoin* rooms employing a utensil stand called a *daisu*. Hideyoshi was interested in all forms of *chanoyu*, and Rikyū was able to satisfy his interests better than the other two masters since he was constantly devising new methods of serving tea or new shapes for tea utensils. Before Rikyū's time, for example, most of the bowls appreciated in the tea ceremony were made in China and thus were not designed specifically for the ceremony. Rikyū was the first to fashion an original bowl especially for serving tea. (An earlier attempt to imitate the *tenmoku* bowls of China was made by potters of Seto in the fourteenth century.) Rikyu's bowls, now known as raku bowls, were a simple earthenware, shaped by hand and fired at low temperatures. He selected red and black for the glaze to go with the green powdered tea, and the weight, shape, and rim were all made according to his specifications.

Similarly, Rikyū developed special utensils from among objects found in every household, such as the bamboo flower vase, and gave them an artistic place in the ceremony of tea.

Rikyū further distinguished himself by being the only tea master invited by Hideyoshi to the Imperial Palace in 1585. It was at this time that Hideyoshi asked the emperor for permission to bestow on Rikyū the honored title of *koji*, or enlightened recluse, so that he might be allowed to enter the palace as Hideyoshi's tutor. And so Rikyū's name was formally changed, as it had been on several occasions during his lifetime.

Rikyū thus advanced from the position of *sadō* to that of Hideyoshi's closest attendant. He obtained a great deal of power from his relationship with Hideyoshi and was frequently called upon by people for special favors, or to attend tea ceremonies. We can see just how much power he had from a letter written by Kyushu daimyo Ōtomo Sōrin containing the comment by Hidenaga (Hideyoshi's brother), that Rikyū would take care of the household matters, and Hidenaga the public matters.

Eventually, it began to seem to Hideyoshi that Rikyū knew too much about household matters, and that he had become insolent. On frequent occasions, Rikyū behaved with arrogance, a trait that could be attributed to the peculiar brand of self-esteem held by the *machi-shū* of Sakai. Hideyoshi was often irritated by Rikyū's clever handling of difficult tasks that were specially intended to humble him. Many anecdotes are recorded about the clashes between these two men, among them the story of Rikyū and his morning glories. Rikyū, who was known throughout the city for his beautiful garden of morning glories, invited Hideyoshi to view them early one morning. But when Hideyoshi arrived, he was surprised to see that all the flowers had been cut, and only when he walked inside the room did he find one morning glory displayed in a vase. Hideyoshi, a proud man by nature, was not amused by his teacher's profundity on this occasion.

In another instance Rikyū recited a poem by Fujiwara no Ietaka that he claimed expressed his own sentiment:

> I would like to show those people
> Looking forward to cherry blossoms

The green grass hidden in the snow
In early spring.

This poem was meant to show Hideyoshi that his slightly gaudy tastes were not in accordance with the simplicity and serenity of his teacher's, and Hideyoshi resented the attempt to tell him so.

In the *Record of Yamanoue Sōji* there is a reference to one particular poem by the Buddhist priest Jichin, that Rikyū always recited to himself:

What a pity it is
That the Pure and Perfect Law
We should keep unstained,
Is by men so frequently
Made a source of worldly gain.

In this poem Rikyū exposed the attitude of those people who used the tea ceremony only as a means of making money. Perhaps these statements were offensive to Hideyoshi, who had done much to promote Rikyū's status as a tea master.

Rikyū's excesses, real and imagined, compounded by a number of rumors that came to Hideyoshi's attention, led the ruler to order the tea master's suicide. The more immediate reasons for this may have been because Rikyū was selling tea articles, an undignified practice, or because he had encouraged his widowed daughter to refuse Hideyoshi's attentions, or perhaps because he had allowed a statue of himself to be erected on one of the gates of Daitoku-ji temple. In this case, it is said that Hideyoshi was so enraged at having to walk underneath Rikyū's statue that he ordered the statue to be beheaded as well. Rikyū's death sentence was seen as penance for having angered his master. In any case, his many enemies, who were jealous of Rikyū's power, saw their objective fulfilled on February 28, 1591, when Rikyū died ceremoniously by his own hand.

Thus the great tea master, who had served Hideyoshi for nine out of his seventy years and Nobunaga for twelve, was forced toward a tragic end. Although it has often been said that Rikyū was responsible for all the rules and rituals of the tea ceremony, it is plain from the historical records that more than one person was involved in the refinement of the art of *chanoyu*. The final form as we know it today owes its origins not only to the masters Jōō and Rikyū, but to the people of Sakai, the samurai lords, and their contemporaries. But there is one major difference between the tea ceremony as performed in the days of Rikyū and later ceremonies that followed. The performances of Rikyū were open to men of all classes without distinction. This freedom did not, unfortunately, survive his death.

Warriors and the Tea Ceremony

Some people claim that it was Furuta Oribe, Rikyū's student, who succeeded him and served Hideyoshi after his death, but it is very uncertain whether this actually occurred or not. According to historical records, two weeks before his death, Rikyū was ordered to return to Sakai and confine himself to his house. Since it was publicly known that Rikyū had been condemned to death, not one of his three thousand students saw him off when he left for Sakai. It is understandable that his students, most of whom were generals and nobles, did not wish to be implicated in his crime and denied having been closely associated with the tea master. There is, however, one letter still in existence that was written by Rikyū to his pupil Matsui Yasuyuki the morning after he reached Sakai. Yasuyuki was chief retainer to Hosokawa Tadaoki, a feudal lord who later became a tea devotee with the name of Sansai. Rikyū's letter thanked Tadaoki and Oribe for secretly coming as far as Yodo to see him off, a calculated risk in those days but an indication of the strong respect that these two men had for Rikyū.

Just before his death, Rikyū instructed his pupils to learn the art of tea from Oribe and to learn the making of tea scoops from Sansai. Rikyū was clearly attached to these two students and taught them many of his own techniques. It is improbable, however, that Oribe, a feudal lord, could have succeeded Rikyū without first resigning from his post, which he did only after Hideyoshi's death. Furthermore, there were several other masters in higher positions who would have been the more natural choice to succeed Rikyū, including Sansai.

It is more likely that Rikyū's post was never filled, for, as we have seen, Hideyoshi quite often conducted the tea ceremony himself. He was also quite capable of planning such gatherings, although he did obtain assistance from experts in organizing them. But, after Rikyū's death, Hideyoshi was reluctant to display his dependence on the *machi-shū* of Sakai, and he refrained from asking for immediate assistance.

It was to the residents of Hakata that he finally turned for support, because he especially needed the political alliance of the merchants of that town. This was because when Hideyoshi defeated the Shimazu clan of Kyushu in 1587, he used Hakata as a base camp. Hakata had been, like Sakai, a self-governing town, whose trade with the merchants of China and Korea had been established in earlier times. Hideyoshi was eager to conquer China and Korea after his unification of Japan, and he needed the knowledge and economic power of the merchants of Hakata. Therefore, he invited Kamiya Sōtan and Shimai Sōshitsu of Hakata to a tea ceremony at his base camp, and treated them as cordially as his predecessor Nobunaga had treated the men of Sakai when he needed their assistance.

Hideyoshi continued to court the merchants of Hakata, especially after he declared war on Korea in 1591 when Korea refused to become an ally in his war with China. This war, which lasted seven years and saw troops dispatched from Japan twice, ended with the death of Hideyoshi and brought about the downfall of the Toyotomi clan. The struggle for control of the country between the Toyotomis and the Tokugawas ended in 1603 with the appointment of Tokugawa Ieyasu as commander-in-chief and shogun. He brought his government to Edo, present-day Tokyo.

In 1599, a year after Hideyoshi's death, Oribe held a tea gathering at Fushimi. Kamiya Sōtan noted Oribe's use of distorted bowls made in the Seto district. Later, in 1610, Oribe is said to have taught *daisu*-style *temae* to Hidetada, Ieyasu's son. At this point, Oribe had acquired a considerable reputation as an eminent tea master in Ieyasu's court. Although Oribe followed the rules laid down by Rikyū, his style differed in many ways from that of his master's. Perhaps their differences in background— Oribe came from the samurai class and Rikyū from the merchant class— could account for their differences in taste.

Rikyū's favorite colors were black and gray, while Oribe liked colors that combined dark green and white, or charcoal gray and scarlet on a white background. These came to be known later as "Oribe colors." Oribe also preferred black ceramics, and his favorite shapes were distorted circles, triangles, and pentagons, quite distinct from the simple square or circle that Rikyū favored. And while Rikyū tried to maintain a tranquil atmosphere in the garden leading to the tea room, undisturbed even by the scent of flowers, Oribe used to have dandelions blooming or doves singing outside his tea house. Rikyū had stressed the value of practicality over beauty, but Oribe contradicted his dictum by placing more emphasis on appearance.

Oribe might have decided to contravene Rikyū's rules on purpose in an effort to please the public, who still regarded Rikyū as a criminal. After the death of Hideyoshi, the tea ceremony underwent more changes, one of the most drastic being its virtual monopoly by the samurai, who looked upon it as a suitable pastime for their class. The Tokugawas especially supported this view, and the hitherto democratic spirit of the tea ceremony was buried along with Hideyoshi.

Now that *chanoyu* was no longer the exclusive practice of the court nobles, more importance came to be placed on its outward forms.

Dignity and decorum correctly observed became the fashion. This had its origins in Confucianism, which the Tokugawas adhered to with fervor, and it resulted in a formal and logical arrangement of people and ideas.

Oribe's career was short-lived, and in 1615, during one of the battles between the Tokugawas and the Toyotomis, he was suspected of spying for the Toyotomis and forced to commit suicide. This put a quick end to his style of tea, which had combined the *shoin* style of the court nobles with Rikyū's simple tea-hut style.

His contemporary, Sansai, did not give lessons, but was a famed collector of tea utensils. An amusing anecdote is told about him. When a certain man asked to see his tea utensils on an appointed day, Sansai decorated the walls of his rooms with the Hosokawa military arms. When asked for an explanation, he replied simply, "I am a warrior, so my principal utensils are weapons of war." Sansai, unlike Oribe, did not attempt to change any of the rules of his teacher.

After Oribe's death, one of his pupils, Kobori Enshū, a feudal lord with a fief of ten thousand *koku* (a traditional unit of measure for grain, particularly rice, equal to 1800 liters / 5 bushels), became famous for his innovations. Enshū was a man of many skills. He had succeeded his father as the magistrate for construction at the age of twenty-six and built castles and palaces. In the historical accounts it is stated that he once danced for a large gathering of distinguished guests at a cherry blossom–viewing party. He had also at one time studied meditation under the Zen priest Shunoku Sōen of Daitoku-ji temple. In this way Enshū was associated with many cultured people and also acquired a broad range of artistic accomplishments. His skill is evident not only in the public buildings he constructed, but also in the tea rooms and gardens around Daitoku-ji that have been carefully preserved until this day.

Among his many accomplishments, Enshū also designed furniture and tea articles distinguished by their dignity and splendor and now referred to as "Enshū-style" pieces. His combination of decorative beauty and simplicity came to be known as *kirei sabi*, and resembled the style preferred by the court nobles that Rikyū had frowned upon. But in calligraphy and poetry, Enshū had the same admiration for Fujiwara no Teika as Rikyū had had, and Enshū selected names for his tea articles from the poems in Fujiwara's *Anthology Collected by Imperial Command*. His style soon became known as the daimyo style, and his fame spread throughout Japan, all the more so after he became *chanoyu* advisor to the shogun himself. Later, many local lords employed Enshū's students as their principal tea masters.

The Nobility and the Literati

During the five years of struggle between the Toyotomi and Tokugawa clans just before the Edo shogunate was established in 1603, the tea ceremony enjoyed great popularity with members of the imperial family and their entourage. The vogue for tea was even reflected in the styles of buildings constructed for them. These included the Katsura Imperial Villa in Kyoto, which had a small section in the Shōkintei building used exclusively for tea ceremonies. The palace was built by two generations of princes, Toshihito and Toshitada, the former of whom was also Hideyoshi's adopted son for a short while. The decoration was elaborate, in the style of tea rooms preferred by the court nobles in the Muromachi period. The Shūgaku-in Imperial Villa, constructed in Kyoto for the former emperor Go-mizunoo also had a *shoin*-style tea room. Similarly, the Minase Shrine, often visited by the emperor, contained a rather splendid room for the tea ceremony.

Perhaps it was Toshihito, Hideyoshi's adopted son, who was responsible for starting up a vogue for tea among members of the imperial family at the end of the sixteenth century. Toshihito had formerly performed *chanoyu* for Hideyoshi, and he later entertained several emperors including Emperor Ōgimachi, although it was Hideyoshi who first introduced the tea ceremony to the imperial court. In this way the tea ceremony came to be known by the most powerful family of regents, the Konoe clan. The tea styles that they enjoyed most were those of the Oribe School and the Kanamori Sōwa School, because Sōwa had associated with emperors in the past, namely Gosai and Go-mizunoo and also the latter's wife, Tōfukumonin.

Sōwa's style of performance was entirely different from the *wabi* style advocated by Rikyū and his followers. He preferred a method that was both aesthetic and aristocratic, which pleased those members of the nobility who studied with him. Inspired by Sōwa, Prince Joshuin began to teach *chanoyu* to aristocrats, among them Konoe Yorakuin, who carried on the prince's style of tea, referring to it as *oryūgi*, or the authentic style of tea. With this distinct break in the form of the tea ceremony, a certain snob appeal arose for the court style of *chanoyu*, which was simultaneously known as the daimyo style.

This created a problem for the educated men and priests who did not feel that they belonged to either group. They therefore formed their own style of the tea ceremony in accordance with their status that was quite close to the daimyo style, since their innovators mingled more with the upper classes. Hon'ami Kōetsu was one such man. Born in 1558, Kōetsu had been a polisher of swords since his youth, but because of his interest in tea, he was a close friend of the tea masters Oribe, Oda Uraku, Enshū, and Sōtan. Kōetsu, who was also a master calligrapher, was awarded a tract of land in Takagamine by Ieyasu in 1615. He retired there with his kinsmen, forming a community based on shared faith in the Nichiren sect of Buddhism, and continued to craft numerous artistic works.

Priests like Shōkadō Shōjō, who served at the Iwashimizu Hachiman Shrine in Kyoto, also had dealings with the court. Shōjō was a noted calligrapher, and during his youth had been employed by Konoe Nobutada, with whom he was very close. Through his connections with the Konoe family and the Owari branch of the Tokugawa, Shōjō sometimes acted as mediator between the shogunate and the Imperial court. Concerning the tea ceremony, his association with Enshū is well known. Other influential *chanoyu* devotees included priests of the Daitoku-ji temple, such as Takuan (1573–1645) and Kōgetsu, son of Sōgyū, who were both friends of Enshū and Shōkadō.

Sen no Sōtan (1578–1658)

Sōtan was an eminent and respected tea master of the *wabi* style, inherited perhaps from his grandfather Rikyū. Sōtan was the son of Shōan, the stepson of Rikyū after his second marriage. In 1591, when Rikyū committed suicide, Sōtan was only fourteen, and was then staying with Rikyū's Zen teacher Shunoku at the Daitoku-ji. Sōtan practiced Zen meditation, not through any desire to enter the priesthood, but in order to acquire basic training in Buddhism.

When permission was granted for restoration of the Sen family, Sōtan returned home and with his father Shōan worked toward the revival of Rikyū's style of tea ceremony. Sōtan took over headship of the family from his father in 1600, and like his father labored under the political burden of Rikyū's forced suicide, holding tea gatherings as a tea master from around 1608.

As a child Sōtan had not acquired Rikyū's taste for the tea ceremony, and since he did not live with him there was little chance that the two men, separated by over half a century in time, would have had much in common in their manner of serving tea. Sōtan actually came under heavy criticism from some of Rikyū's students who were still alive during that time, and especially from members of the Oribe School, whose form of tea ceremony was based on Rikyū's style. Their main contention was that "Sōtan's tea ceremony was created through his own will and differed from the way that Rikyū taught." It was fairly obvious that Rikyū had made a firm impression on his followers and his style was regarded as the yardstick for all tea devotees.

Although the tea ceremony flourished as a pastime of feudal lords,

Sōtan's personal life was one of poverty and simple frugality. He never worked for a feudal lord, presumable because he wished to avoid the dangers that befell his grandfather. His letters, however, indicate that he pushed for his sons to enter into service. Discord between him and Sōsetsu, his elder son, is said to have risen out of Sōsetsu's lack of enthusiasm for the idea of working for a feudal lord. By sending his children to officiate at tea ceremonies for feudal lords, by reestablishing the Sen family on a firm basis, and by training four highly renowned tea masters, Sōtan laid the foundations for the preservation of Rikyū's style of tea for future generations.

One of his pupils, Yamada Sōhen, who started *chanoyu* at age of six and began lessons under Sōtan at eighteen, later founded the Sōhen School of Tea. Sōhen was the heir to the Chōtoku-ji temple, but he was so impressed by his teacher that he gave up his honored position at the age of twenty-six to devote himself to tea. There is one anecdote that is very revealing of Sōtan's character. After his decision to become a tea devotee, Sōhen took on his mother's family name and went to live in a small hut in Narutaki, near Kyoto. One day, the chief priest of Hongan-ji temple was to visit Sōhen, and Sōtan, hearing that such a distinguished person was going to see his pupil, rushed over to Sōhen's hut with a water jar and a pair of tongs that had once belonged to his grandfather. He gave his student suggestions as to how to conduct the ceremony, and before the guest arrived Sōtan hid himself behind a screen to give last-minute advice.

Another instance of Sōtan's attempts to establish Sōhen's career as *sadō* occurred when he sent him in his place to perform for the daimyo Ogasawara and become his tea master. Sōhen served Ogasawara so ably that he became the tea master to the family for forty-three years. Sōhen also published several volumes detailing the Sōtan tradition of *wabicha*, a simple style of tea.

Sōtan's style of serving tea was also much admired by Sugiki Fusai, another pupil, who was a Shinto priest at Ise Shrine. One of Fusai's duties as a priest was to organize pilgrimages to Ise Shrine. Traveling around the Kinki district, he spread the ideas of Sōtan, which differed from the more flamboyant styles of the Oribe and Enshū schools prominent at the time. Above all, Fusai attempted to keep alive the *wabi* tradition, which emphasized simplicity through Zen spirituality.

Katagiri Sekishū (1605–73)

Like Sōtan before him, Sekishū was in favor of classic simplicity in tea performances. He was a daimyo and the magistrate of construction for the Tokugawas, as Enshū had been, and later he was also seen as the natural successor to Enshū as leader of tea ceremony for the warrior class. He studied the art of tea with Kuwayama Sōsen, pupils of Dōan, the oldest son of Rikyū.

While he was still practicing Zen meditation at the Daitoku-ji under the guidance of Gyokushitsu Sōhaku, he wrote an important essay on the spirit of tea called *An Essay on Wabi (Sekishū Wabi no Fumi)*. Sekishū followed Rikyū's style, but not in the same way as the Sōtan and Oribe schools, for he felt that a warrior should behave in a certain manner befitting his rank. He borrowed some of Jōō's principles that were more accommodating to rigid social distinctions, and later wrote down his ideas in a book called *Sekishū's Three Hundred Articles*.

Sekishū's style was influenced by the social conditions of his time, and since the Tokugawas ruled the country, the formal daimyo style was seen to be most suitable for the warrior class. The adoption of Sekishū's style of tea by the Tokugawa shogunate caused it to spread widely among the feudal lords. However, it should not be forgotten that Rikyū's descendants also served as tea instructors to daimyo families.

The Establishment of Different Tea Schools

It had been customary since the Heian period in the ninth century for an art to be handed down from one generation to another in the family, to secure its purity. These "houses," with officially recognized skills, were called *iemoto*. But at the beginning of Tokugawa rule in the seventeenth century, the government had a policy that the eldest son of a family, whether shogun, lord, or merchant, should always succeed his father. The word *iemoto* later came to refer especially to the head of a school of traditional arts. Under the *iemoto* system of succession a person's lineage came to be more highly regarded than his capability or skill.

With the acceptance of the *iemoto* system, Senke, Enshū, and other schools came to be known by the family name of their originator.

The Senke School of Tea, named after the family name of Sen no Sōtan, was the chief opponent of the Sekishū School. Sōtan's second son, Sōshu, was the chief tea master for the Takamatsu family; Sōsa, the third son, served the Tokugawas in the Kishū district; and Sōshitsu, the youngest, was on friendly terms with the Maeda clan. All three sons lived and worked in Kyoto, giving lessons to the wealthy merchants there, who were increasingly being made to feel socially inferior if they were not well versed in the art of tea.

During this time the Edo administration was becoming more politically stable, and the rule of the samurai gave way to a new system of economic control by the merchant class. As this class came to play a more dominant role in society, the tea ceremony once more reverted to a mere pastime for the rich. Tea articles were bought and sold, and marks of authenticity by the more famous masters increased the commercial value of these objects.

As far as the Senke School was concerned, however, the art was passed on by Sōtan to his sons, who devoted themselves solely to the cult of tea, unlike the former daimyo tea masters Enshū and Sekishū, who practiced tea as a hobby. And in keeping with the prevalent taste in architecture of the times, which was for a more lavish drawing-room style, the Senke School also moved away from the rigid simplicity of Sōtan toward a looser, more aesthetic style. The Senke School patronized new teachers according to the *iemoto* system, and men like Joshinsai Tennen, Ittō Sōshitsu, and Kawakami Fuhaku (who founded the Edosenke School) helped formulate the *Seven Training Exercises of the Tea Ceremony*, the *Shichijishiki*, a set of procedures which gives the student practice in all elements of tea and some peripheral practices such as incense appreciation.

After Sōtan's death in 1658, his school was divided by his three sons, who each started their own school, named according to the area in which it was situated. Sōshu called his school the Mushanokōjisenke, after the street by that name in Kyoto; Sōsa called his the Omotesenke, as it was situated at the front of the property; and Sōshitsu, who inherited the rear of the property, called his school Urasenke.

Matsudaira Fumai and Ii Naosuke

The Sekishū School was popular among the feudal lords because of a rule that allowed a student to receive qualifications to teach the tea ceremony once they had completed a course. The Senke School was far more severe when it came to the question of teaching, so many lords preferred the freer method of the Sekishū School. Two students of Sekishū developed their own observations and criticisms of the tea ceremony and published important works on the art.

One of them was Matsudaira Fumai (1751–1818), lord of the small town of Matsue, who published a criticism of tea at the age of twenty called *Idle Talk*. He attacked the extravagance of tea performances that ignored the sensitivities and spirituality of the special tea aesthetic. Later he became an avid collector of tea articles, for he feared that such works of art would perish if they were not carefully preserved. In the 1787 preface of his *Collection of Valuable Articles from Ancient and Modern Times*,

Fumai gave very detailed descriptions of famous tea bowls, tea caddies, and ancient silks that belonged to the daimyo families of his period. This is one of the earliest illustrated catalogs of tea articles ever published, and he divides his study into three periods, pre-Rikyū, Rikyū, and post-Rikyū.

Fumai also wrote down his own observations on the conduct of the tea ceremony in a book called the *Foundation of the Tea Cult*, where he attributed great responsibility to the role of the host: "The host is responsible for any mistakes the guest makes. He should entertain the guest flexibly according to the mood of the occasion. If the host sticks too closely to formalities and principles, his service can only be regarded as unrefined and in bad taste."

Ii Naosuke (1815–1860) is also known by his tea name of Sōkan. He was the fourteenth child of the lord of Hikone, and when his father died he was forced to live alone in a separate house in the heart of the city. He was then seventeen, and to relieve boredom he took up the study of Buddhism, classical literature, and poetry, as well as *chanoyu*. When his brothers died, he found himself leader of the clan, and at the age of forty-four he was offered the important office of chief minister by the Tokugawa government. He is also well known as the minister who signed the Commercial Treaty with the United States in 1858.

Sōkan conducted detailed research on the history of tea and wrote prolifically on the spiritual and utilitarian practices involved in the tea ceremony. He maintained that the spirit of tea was necessary for the rulers of the country, and although he himself belonged to the daimyo class, he said that his idea of the tea ceremony belonged to the distant age of Rikyū and Sakai, when *chanoyu* was simple and accessible to all.

NOTES

1. Oda Nobunaga, a valiant and resolute warrior, almost brought the whole of Japan under his rule to end the period of civil wars, but was attacked by his retainer Akechi Mitsuhide in 1582 and forced to commit suicide before he could achieve this.

2. During the Muromachi and Azuchi-Momoyama periods, inhabitants of self-governing cities were referred to by this name.

3. Fujiwara no Teika (1162–1241), a famous poet, scholar, and calligrapher of the Kamakura period, compiled the two well-known anthologies entitled *Shinkokin-waka-shū* and *Shinchokusen-waka-shū*.

4. The first rifle to arrive in Japan was brought by Portuguese on board a Chinese ship that drifted ashore at Tanegashima (Kagoshima Prefecture) in 1543.

5. Toyotomi Hideyoshi (1536–98) served under Oda Nobunaga and rose from being a foot soldier to become ruler of Japan in the Azuchi-Momoyama period. He defeated Mitsuhide, his chief opponent, at the battle of Yamazaki, after which he conquered the areas of Japan that had not been brought under control by Nobunaga. In 1585 he became chief advisor to the emperor. He fell ill in 1597 during a campaign against Korea and died a year later.

6. Akechi Mitsuhide (1528–82) was a warrior in the service of Nobunaga. He was humiliated by his master and retaliated by attacking Nobunaga at Honnō-ji temple in Kyoto and forcing him to commit suicide. Thirteen days later, Mitsuhide himself was defeated at Yamazaki by Hideyoshi.

7. This famous battle, fought in Kyoto between Hideyoshi and Mitsuhide for control of the country after the forced suicide of Nobunaga, ended in June 1582, with the victory of Hideyoshi.

8. Gold and silver mines were discovered in Japan in the sixteenth century, and as a result, tea utensils of that period came to include items made from these precious metals.

9. In the Azuchi and Momoyama periods, tea masters who served samurai and daimyo lords were known by this name. In the Edo period, a *sadō* was a tea master who served the Tokugawas and was usually rewarded with a fief.

10. *Ranjatai* is the name given to a large piece of aromatic wood brought from China that has been stored in the Shōsō-in, the Imperial Treasure House, since the eighth century. Nobunaga obtained a very small piece of it in 1574.

Tea bowl called *Yugure* (Dusk) attributed to Chōjirō. Red raku ware, Momoyama period, Japan. The bowl was originally named by Sen no Sōtan.

NOTE: The pieces shown in this and the following fifteen color plates repre-
sent highlights from the collection of the Goto Museum in Tokyo, home to
one of the most renowned collections of tea utensils in Japan.

Tea bowl called *Akujo* (Shameless Woman) attributed to Jōkei. Black raku ware, Momoyama period, Japan. The name is thought to come from the deep, wide recess in the base of the bowl, which apparently reminded the owner of the "depth of wanton passion" of shameless women.

Tea bowl called *Waraya* (Thatch Hut). Black glaze, Mino ware, Momoyama period, Japan. Oribe-type bowls are characterized by their asymmetrical shape and abstract pattern. The name *Waraya* is written next to the foot of the bowl in lacquer in Sen no Sōtan's own hand.

Tea bowl called *Kuchiki*, after Kuchiki Tanemasa (1643–1714), the daimyo who owned it. Hakuan-type, locquat-colored, Edo period, Japan or Korea.

Tea bowl called *Mino*, Ido-type, glazed ceramic, Li dynasty, Korea.

Container for thick tea called *Anko-kuji* after being passed on by the Hosokawa daimyo family to Ankokuji Ekei (?–1600), a priest in the Momoyama period. Glazed ceramic, Southern Sung dynasty, China.

Container for thick tea in an eggplant shape, called *Sōgo*, after its first owner, Jūshiya Sōgo, who was active at the end of the Azuchi-Momoyama period. Glazed ceramic, Southern Sung dynasty, China.

Container for thick tea called *Rikyū Enza*. Glazed ceramic, Southern Sung dynasty, China. The name of this piece derives from two disparate facts: it was owned by Sen no Rikyū and its base resembles an *enza*, a circular cushion made of woven straw.

Drawstring pouches accompanying the *Rikyū Enza* tea container.

Ashiya kettle (made in what is now Fukuoka Prefecture, Kyūshū) in conventional *shin* shape, with design of lions and peonies. Cast iron, Muromachi period, Japan.

Ashiya kettle in conventional *shin* shape, with fine "hailstone" surface, once owned by Sen no Rikyū. Cast iron, Muromachi period, Japan. The base was damaged from years of use and has been replaced.

Water jar called *Yabure Bukuro* (Burst Pouch). Old Iga ware, natural ash-glazed stoneware, Momoyama period, Japan. This classic tea piece received its present name after it was designated an Important Cultural Asset in 1955. In earlier documents it is referred to as the *Kagogata Mizusashi* (Basket-shaped Jar).

Water jar referred to as *Bō no Saki Mizusashi* (Palanquin-pole-end Water Jar). Brass alloy, seventeenth century, China. Representative of brass alloy products imported from China in this period, this type of jar was known in Japan as *namban-sahari*, and was mainly employed as a vase and waste-water receptacle.

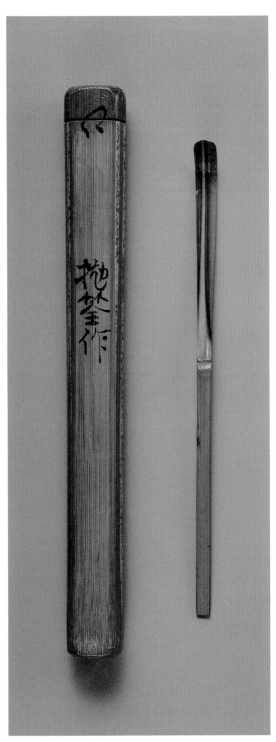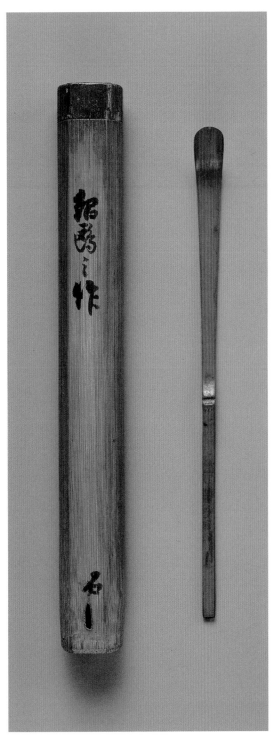

Tea scoop, with inserted piece at back, by Sen no Rikyū. Bamboo with container inscribed by Kobori Enshū with the phrase "Hōsen saku." Momoyama period, Japan. "Hōsen" was another name for Rikyū. This utensil is one of the tea master's most renowned tea scoops.

Tea scoop by Takeno Jōō. Bamboo with container inscription by Katagiri Sekishū, Momoyama period, Japan. Few tea scoops by Jōō survive, and this one is especially unusual in that it has the bamboo joint in the center, a feature that was originally thought to have been conceived after Sen no Rikyū's time.

Vase, with phoenix ears, *kinuta*-type *lung-chuan* celadon. Porcelain, Southern Sung Dynasty, China. Important Cultural Property.

Vase called *Ō-sorori*, with elongated neck and shape. Bronze alloy, Southern Sung Dynasty, China.

White camellia and Japanese allspice (*rōbai*) in a simple bamboo hanging vase. The white glow of the camellia adds a refreshing touch to the tea room in the deepening cold of winter.

Black lilies in a celadon vase: fresh clean lines for spring.

Water images for midsummer: clematis in a boat-shaped vase suspended from the ceiling. The vase is named *Tanabata*, after the "Star Festival" in July.

"Cuckoo" lilies with autumn grasses in a bamboo basket shaped like a cormorant fisherman's creel.

Red camellia and pine in a bronze vase of indeterminate age. Pine, the symbol of long life, and camellia, for its purity, are favorites for New Year.

After filling the stone water basin with fresh water, the host greets the guests in silence. They then proceed to the stone basin and wash their hands and rinse out their mouths before entering the tea room.

Guests partake of a *kaiseki* meal. After finishing, they will leave the tea room while the host prepares the room for the thick-tea ceremony.

A full *kaiseki* meal starts with small servings of rice, miso soup, and a delicacy such as raw fish (all seen on the tray in the foreground), served with saké. This is followed by *nimono*, the main course, which is vegetables, dumplings, fish and/or tofu served in a clear soup (pictured to the right of the tray). Separate dishes of something grilled, boiled, and vinegared are then served one at a time, followed by lightly flavored hot water (in lacquered cups with lids) to refresh the palate. *Hassun*, tiny servings of something choice from the mountains and the sea, is brought out with more saké. The meal ends with rice and pickles.

The main guest accepts a bowl of thick tea from the host.

II

THE AESTHETIC

Aesthetics of Tea

The Spirit of *Chanoyu*

A lot of the misunderstanding of the art of the tea ceremony stems from the mistaken impression that it is the purely physical act of making and drinking tea, a pleasant pastime in which a beverage is enjoyed. However, this is only the superficial aspect of the tea ceremony. What cannot easily be observed is the spiritual side of the ceremony implied in the name *chanoyu*. Besides the very disciplined frame of mind that is a prerequisite for performing tea, there is a special code of ethics shared by the host and guests that makes *chanoyu* a distinctly Japanese art.

The first tea master of the past to emphasize the spiritual aspect of the tea ceremony was Shukō, who taught to the importance of the right frame of mind. He claimed that purity of mind, rather than a superficial appearance of cleanliness, should be aimed for at all times. In relations between the host and his guests, self-restraint and consideration are the key attributes, and a person of a lower social status should be given the same degree of respect as one who comes from a high social level.

Shukō's ideas were diligently followed by Jōō, who expanded his teacher's ideas in the book *Chanoyusha no Kakugo Juttai*, setting down the proper mental attitude while performing the tea ceremony. The tea master's skill, he added, would be enhanced by correct daily conduct with other people, that is without affectation or arrogance.

These ideas also coincided with Rikyū's, whose words show that he had a great understanding of the deeper spiritual nature of *chanoyu*. Once when he was asked about the proper conduct of the host and guest, he answered simply that it is correct for the host to do his best to please his guest, but incorrect to make a fuss about doing so. Unfortunately, Rikyū's simple and unaffected style could not be practiced while he was in the service of Hideyoshi.

After Rikyū's death, the art of *chanoyu* was taken over by daimyo lords who pursued it as a means of respite from their political lives and as a form of recreation befitting their role in society. Nevertheless, Rikyū's influence during his lifetime helped to preserve the purity and simplicity of the tea ceremony from deterioration into a mere fashionable pastime for the feudal chiefs. Even Enshū, though he did not receive Rikyū's personal teaching, refused to be entertained with food cooked without sincerity or to drink tea from bowls that did not reflect the simplicity (*wabi*) that Rikyū emphasized.

One of Enshū's successors, Katagiri Sekishū, a feudal lord himself, wrote a book called *An Essay on Wabi* (*Sekishū Wabi no Fumi*). He described two types of tea masters: one who loves the formality of the ceremony, the elegance of the atmosphere, and the beauty of the utensils; and the true tea devotee who loves the spirituality of the ceremony. Sekishū pointed out that the essence of the *wabi* style of tea can be found in a one-and-a-half-mat room. His ideas clearly differed from the daimyo style of *chanoyu* that was being practiced, but since he himself was a daimyo, he had no choice but to teach a style of conduct befitting the student's social standing, which was contrary to Rikyū's idea of the importance of equality in the tea room.

Rikyū's philosophy, however, was put into practice by his grandson, Sōtan, and Sōtan's students. Sōtan, as we know, led a life of austerity, shunning fame and riches, in the pursuit of truth. Gradually, as he won the respect of the people around him, some of the most famous tea masters of his time began to spread his teachings on *wabi*. In his writings Sōtan deplored the degeneration of *chanoyu*, which had become merely a pastime for displaying wealth. Sōtan's style of tea was described as sordid while Sōwa's style was considered elegant.

After Sōtan's death, his students were appointed chief tea masters to various daimyo families, but they were unable to perpetuate the simple *wabi* style of Sōtan, because it was felt that daimyo deserved a more exalted style. Meanwhile, in merchant circles, the tea ceremony was being passed on to wealthy individuals who were increasingly ignorant of the true spirit of *wabi* and who performed tea according to their own uninitiated styles.

Some feudal lords like Matsudaira Fumai, who had studied the Seki-shū style of tea, talked about the degeneration of *chanoyu*. In his books he pointed out that the ceremony had diverged too greatly from its original theory and was being performed willy-nilly. Tea masters only talked of *wabi* but did not put it into practice. He called for a return to the original concept of tea, since mere mastery of ritual was insufficient if the basic rapport between host and guest remained undeveloped. In like manner, Ii Naosuke, author of the well-known book on tea *Chanoyu Ichie-shū*, described the ceremonies of his time as lacking in proper communication between host and guest.

The tea ceremony seemed to have lost forever the humble *wabi* style as it progressed from the time of Shukō to Naosuke, despite Fumai's warning against an excessive display of materialism in the ceremony. Not until the latter half of the nineteenth century, when Okakura Kakuzō (or Tenshin) wrote *The Book of Tea* in English, was another attempt made to capture the elusive "spirit" of tea. He said:

> Tea with us became more than an idealization of the form of
> drinking; it is a religion of the art of life. The beverage grew to
> be an excuse for the worship of purity and refinement, a sacred
> function at which the host and guest joined to produce for that
> occasion the utmost beatitude of the mundane. The tea-room
> was an oasis in the dreary waste of existence where weary
> travellers could meet to drink from the common spring of art-
> appreciation.

Thus the intricacy of thought behind the tea ceremony is expressed, without which the essence of the performance is lost.

Wabi and Other Terms in the Tea Ceremony

The literal translation of *wabi* is loneliness or desolation, and it infers the simplicity and tranquility inherent in the state of loneliness or desolation. In the middle of the Muromachi period, two other words were coined to mean simplicity and tranquility—*hiekareru* and *kajikeru*—and they have come to be used interchangeably with *wabi*.

The term *hiekareru* in the tea ceremony was defined by Shukō, who applied it to masters who not only owned beautiful utensils, but had the ability to truly appreciate their beauty. He denounced the trend to use Bizen and Shigaraki pottery by those who had no real understanding of their artistic value. He used the term *hiekareru* for people who practiced tea with an understanding of the true aesthetic and who had become more discriminating in the types of tea articles they used. It was not until later, at the end of the Muromachi period, that the expression *wabi-suki* was used in place of *hiekareru*.

For a *wabi-suki* style to be correctly effected, the tea master ideally lived a life of seclusion in the countryside, where his inner quietude could not be disturbed by worldly matters. It was said that a life without embellishments of any kind was the ultimate means of attaining spiritual wealth. Buddhism said that one may lead a life of detachment without going as far as to become a hermit. This concept greatly influenced the merchants of Sakai, who found they could detach themselves from their daily commercial activities through the practice of *chanoyu*.

It is also said that the man who believes implicitly in *wabi-suki* casts away everything that is unnecessary except for what is vital for practical living. To observers from the outside, such a life may seem miserable, but for the true adherent, it is the attainment of a peaceful frame of mind in the transience of the temporal world. Very few men, it seems, could put this ideal into practice, and in the *Record of Yamanoue Sōji* Shukō speaks of only one master, Zenpō of Awataguchi, who was a true follower of *wabi-suki*.

Rikyū's tea incorporated the idea of *wabi*, and his pursuit of the *wabi* ideal could be found in his invention of the one-and-a-half–mat tea room, where *chanoyu* could be performed with more spirituality than in a larger room. His love of dark, somber colors such as gray and black, and his preference for rough raku tea bowls typify the *wabi* spirit. But Rikyū was unable to practice this ideal to the fullest while he served the powerful rulers Nobunaga and Hideyoshi. Nevertheless, he did teach the *wabi* style to his students. He regretted the state of affairs in which he had to contravene his ideals to stay alive, and often consoled himself with Fujiwara's poem (see Tea Masters and Tea styles).

The meaning of *wabi* underwent a change during the Edo period, when the poet Matsuo Bashō used the word *wabi* to explain his idea on haiku. There is another word, *iki*, that was popular during that time and was thought to describe the characteristics of Edo culture along with *wabi*, but *iki* has connotations of luxury hidden in its meaning and stems from a kind of epicurism. The concept of *wabi* is exceptionally difficult, even to the Japanese, to fully comprehend. Although *wabi* utensils are easy to appreciate, it is not so easy to come to terms with the full depth of *wabi* spirituality.

Zen Philosophy and the Tea Ceremony

It was the Zen priest Eisai who first brought the idea of drinking pow-dered green tea to Japan and encouraged tea-drinking among his fellow priests. He is believed to have planted tea bushes around his temple in an effort to achieve this end while he spread Zen teachings. Since the first teachers of tea were Zen priests, the connection between Zen and tea was unavoidable. Many of the preparations involved in tea are a reflection of Zen thought, and in later days the expression was coined that "Zen and Tea are one and the same." Yamanoue Sōji went even further, saying that since *chanoyu* derived from Zen, it was obligatory for all tea masters to study the philosophy. Shukō, the father of the tea ceremony, studied Zen under the monk Ikkyū of Daitoku-ji temple. Yōsō Sōi, a disciple of Kasō Sōdon under whom Ikkyū studied Zen, spread the religion to the merchants of Sakai. He was so popular among them, the Yōshun-an, an early example of a Zen temple, was built in Sakai for him.

The close ties between the merchants of Sakai and the Zen priests were further cemented when two wealthy Sakai merchants, Takeno Jōō and Kitamuki Dōchin, both well-known tea masters, studied Zen under Dairin Sōtō, who had been one of Rikyū's tutors. His other teachers were the priests Shōrei Shōkin and Kokei Sōchin.

When Daitoku-ji had to be restored after being partly destroyed in the civil wars, it was the merchants of Sakai who helped to finance the project. It soon became the custom to appoint one abbot for both Daitoku-ji and Nanshū-ji, and each time this occurred the merchants donated a substantial sum to both. This interdependence between priests and the *machi-shū* made it easy for many merchants and their sons to become priests at Daitoku-ji. One such person was Sengaku Sōdō, younger brother of the merchant Tani Sōrin. The thirteenth abbot of Nanshū-ji and the 156th of Daitoku-ji was Kōgetsu Sōgan, the son of Tsuda Sōgyū. Chiefly as a result of the spiritual and financial interchange between these two classes of people, many merchants who were tea devotees began to learn Zen, even when they had no intention of entering religious life.

Another factor linking Zen and *chanoyu* is the development of the fine arts of calligraphy, painting, and pottery. The first scrolls (*kakemono*) to hang in the tea room alcove were specimens of highly prized calligraphy executed by the Sung and Yuan priests of China. These scrolls were also hung in Zen temples, for the priests had great respect for the Chinese Zen monks. Rikyū began to decorate his tea room with his teacher Kokei's calligraphy, a great honor for Kokei since it was usual at the time for calligraphy only to be displayed posthumously. Later as the popularity of the tea ceremony increased, *chagake*, or "tea scrolls," were made for the tea room. Included among these were the *ichigyōsho*, which contained a single line calligraphy, and the *ji-gasan*, a scroll painting with commentary by the painter.

The close affinity between Zen teachings and the tea ceremony helped mold the rules and rituals of *chanoyu*, and the simplicity and purity inherent in the religion influenced the form that the tea ceremony took. In effect, the same harmony of mind attained upon entering a Zen temple could now be achieved in the serene atmosphere that pervaded the tea room.

The love of the tea ceremony among the priests resulted in the building of many smaller temples in the precincts of the Daitoku-ji where tea gatherings could be held. A good many priests developed a profound aesthetic sense and collected beautiful tea utensils, which later became valuable tea items. Tea was not, however, a practice common at all temples. Many abbots frowned on the tea ceremony, believing it to be a frivolity of the wealthy, and they disliked their priests participating in it.

In my opinion, although there is a very close relationship between the ethics of the Zen religion and *chanoyu*, they differ in the following manner: while Zen calls for enlightenment of the individual through meditation and detachment, *chanoyu* is first an art of communication between people, undertaken in the Zen spirit of sincerity and purity of mind.

Harmony with Nature

Harmony with nature is the basis of *chanoyu*, for it is regarded by its originators as the ultimate means of awakening aesthetic appreciation. The special styles of tea houses and gardens are an indication of this ideal, and unlike Western homes and gardens, which are for the most part built to stand apart from nature, Japanese tea rooms and gardens are designed to blend in with their surroundings.

Tea houses can be made from wooden logs with their bark still intact, or from unpolished wooden pillars bent naturally with age. Their walls are plastered with mud. In the gardens, natural stones are used to build

TEA ROOM
Four-and-a-half-mat tea room showing the different levels of ceiling. The fire pit has been covered up and the portable brazier is out for the warmer months.

paths and rock gardens, and some tea arbors seemed to be built next to trees, as if to give the impression of a more rustic setting. The weather, the movement of the sun, and the change in seasons all play a major role in the interplay between the tea ceremony and nature.

The Japanese have always observed nature very closely, and their preoccupation with the changing of the seasons can be observed in the oldest anthology of poems compiled at the end of the Nara period, the *Manyōshū*. Those who found aesthetic enjoyment in the tea ceremony also possessed great sensitivity to nature, which is probably why obser-vance of the passing of the seasons became such an important part of the art. A significant part of the ritual lies in varying the tea utensils, flowers, cakes, the ingredients of the tea meal (*kaiseki*), and so on, in accordance with the season or the occasion.

It is appropriate here to give a brief description of these changes based on nature. The season for *chanoyu* may be said to begin in Novem-ber, when fresh tea leaves picked in May and set to mature in large pot-tery urns are at last ready to be ground for tea. Moreover, the onset of cold weather brings the opening of the fire pit, or sunken hearth. Cutting the seal on the tea urn is a solemn rite known as *kuchikiri*. To ready the tea house for guests, the tea master sees to it that tatami mats are replaced, the *shōji* screens are repapered, new green bamboo fences are put up in the garden, and bamboo water pipes are refurbished. During this very formal season of the year, the tea ceremony is conducted with the utmost dignity and solemnity.

December marks the year's end. As the year draws to a close, the host selects tea articles that are rather more sedate, in keeping with the general mood of pensiveness and contemplation. On December 31, the *joyagama* (last boiling of the kettle for the year) is celebrated in a spirit of thanks-giving.

Early in January, it is customary for fellow devotees of tea, or students and their master, to get together to celebrate the boiling of the first kettle of water for the New Year, or *hatsugama*. This observance has grown increasingly popular in recent years. Special decorations include large wreaths of braided willow, a hanging scroll appropriate to the season, and an auspicious arrangement of lobster, citrus, and seaweed set on a tray in the alcove.

The beginning of February marks the start of spring under the old lunar calendar, but temperatures are still chilly and the morning sun is slow to rise. An early morning ceremony called *akatsuki* is often celebrated at this time. Participants file into the tea house in the bitter cold and blackness of the hours before sunrise, which takes place just as the *kaiseki* meal is finishing.

March is occasion to celebrate the arrival of spring, around the time when plum blossoms come out early in the month. Tea things connected to the Dolls' Festival of March 3 are often used.

For ceremonies in April, when the cherry trees bloom, tea implements are organized around a theme of cherry blossoms, and in the alcove there may hang a scroll painting inscribed with an ancient *waka* in tribute to the beauty of flowering cherries. But the blossoms soon scatter, and after they are gone, they cannot be made the focus of a tea ceremony until the following year.

April is also the last month when the sunken hearth is used. As the month draws to a close, the host introduces a tone of quiet simplicity into his tea ceremony.

In May, the portable charcoal brazier (*furo*) is brought out and the sunken hearth closed off. If November is the month when winter is ushered in with the serving of new powdered tea, May is the month when cool and refreshing gatherings signal the approach of summer. Called *shoburo* (first brazier), the occasion is observed with due solemnity.

In June, as the temperature and humidity both climb, simplified indoor gatherings called *yūzari* are held in the evenings.

July and August are the two hottest months of the year, when tea ceremonies are often held early in the day, before temperatures get out of hand. Guests are seated before six a.m., enjoying a simple meal followed by a cup of tea. The entire ceremony, known as *asacha* (morning tea), is over in some ninety minutes.

In September, the month of autumn grasses and flowers, the morning and evenings are once again pleasantly cool. Formal tea ceremonies may be held indoors, but many people also choose to perform *chanoyu* outdoors (*nodate*).

In October, as autumn foliage deepens in color, the essential loneliness of the season also makes itself felt. In keeping with the changes of the season, sober-colored tea articles are favored. Tea gatherings held at this juncture, before the serving of new tea in November, are known as *nagori no cha* (leave-taking tea). Traditionally, they are occasion to bid farewell to the waning autumn, while drinking the last of the year's *matcha*.

The choice of appropriate tea utensils is important in creating a suitable mood for each season described above. The emphasis in earlier tea ceremonies tended toward the precious and the luxurious, but as the spiritual essence of the event came to be understood, a taste for simplicity prevailed. Masters like Konparu Zenpō were influential in this regard, and in his *Essay on Sarugaku* he had this to say: "A tea ceremony performed with a bronze brazier, kettle, and water jar may be splendid, but it leaves no deep impression on the soul. But if rough earthenware from Ise or Bizen is used, the soul will be satisfied." This is the kind of profound, aesthetic sentiment that the tea utensils are supposed to instill in the beholder.

The individual beauty of each utensil must also blend harmoniously with all the other utensils needed for the ritual and they are in turn selected according to the occasion or the time of year. Time, place and rank must all be considered when choosing the flowers, scroll, and kettle for the tearoom. Time refers to a consideration of the season in which the tea ceremony is being held and the purpose of the occasion. Place refers to choosing articles in consideration of the size and atmosphere of the room. Finally, the rank of the tea articles should be appropriate to the location and the kind of ceremony that is being given.

It would not be appropriate, for instance, to choose a scroll of a favorite summer scene for a winter tea ceremony. But in rare cases, and when done by a very skilled tea master, a painting showing snow and ice, or a piece of calligraphy expressing cold-weather scenes, can inspire a feeling of coolness in the hot summer.

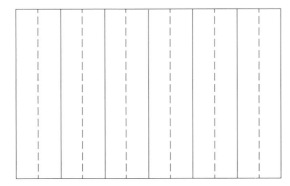

The harmonious arrangement of tea utensils depends a great deal on variety in the shapes of the different vessels used. Unlike the Western habit of using matching cups or bowls in sets, Japanese discover charm in variety; in having no two articles that are exactly the same. If a tall tea caddy is used, it will be balanced by a flat water jar, and a round kettle is best on a square brazier.

At times the tea master will even avoid using two articles produced in the same region or made of the same material. Such an overlap (*tsuku*) might be regarded as carelessness on the part of the master. On the other hand, it is permissible to use three articles that come from the same district since it would be clear that the tea master did this for a reason. Four would be excessive.

Antique utensils dating from the Muromachi period are still used today for formal ceremonies. Articles produced during the Edo period are considered contemporary pieces, and are often harmoniously combined with antique items.

Tea articles with "*mei*" (poetic names) also have a special place in the tea ceremony. A *mei* is given to any favorite item owned by the tea master. This goes back to early days when highly prized utensils would be given *mei* by their owners. Now, however, the word is applied to any scoop or bowl that is a particular favorite. The use of different *mei* together can help to express a season or theme, and also gives the ceremony a more personal flavor as opposed to using articles that are formally regarded as correct for a particular season or occasion.

And lastly, there is the decoration of the tea room itself, which is an important reflection of harmony with nature. In historical times, the *dōbōshū* of the shogun Ashikaga would hang two or three scrolls in the alcove of the *shoin* tea room. They developed a fundamental principle in the use of wall space based on the Chinese theory of *yin* and *yang*, in determining the correct spacing between the scrolls and the height of the scrolls in relation to the length of the room. They called their theory *kanewari.* According to the *kanewari* principle the wall space is divided into six sections by drawing five lines. In the middle of each of the six sections they drew one line; the first five lines were considered *yang*, or positive; and the other six lines drawn in later were *yin*, or negative. This rule was also applied to the placement of the shelves in the side alcove, the design of the stationery desk in *shoin* rooms, and the arrangement of tea utensils, and was incorporated into the aesthetics of the tea ceremony. In practical terms it meant that the number of utensils placed in the main alcove must never be the same as those in the side alcove, and if the former are even in number, then the latter must be odd in number, otherwise the *yin-yang* balance between the two sections would be disturbed.

The Creative Mind
Although harmony and aesthetic sensibility are both necessary in the art of the tea ceremony, the entire arrangement will not be successful without the application of the creative sense known as *hataraki*. Without *hataraki* the act of preparing and serving tea becomes dull and prosaic. In the *Record of Yamanoue Sōji* (in which this creativity is known as *sakubun*), there are two sides to *chanoyu*: the observation of tradition and the employing of creativity. In the *Book of Tea* written in 1600 by Sōshunō, the author states that while a certain conservatism is necessary, the ceremony should not lack in originality or become stiff and static.

The historical records of *chanoyu* gatherings show how this sense of creativity has evolved. In early times, the custom was to begin the tea ceremony after the room had been decorated with all the adornments and the meal served. Some time later, a small change was made, and the alcove was only filled with a few chosen items. The host would bring in the other articles as the ceremony progressed. Later, the guests were invited to rest in the tea garden while the host changed the arrangement of the tea room, and then prepared the thick tea after they returned. With each stage an element of freshness was introduced into the ceremony.

The creativity of a host was expressed in the originality of his choice of decorations for the tea room and tea utensils. There are many anecdotes about the display of flowers in the alcove, and aside from the influence of Buddhist tradition, flower arrangement developed hand in hand with the advancement of the tea ceremony.

An anecdote illustrating the origins of *hataraki* is told by Matsuya Hisamasa, who was invited to a gathering given by Jōō in 1542. In those days it was customary to display many items in a ceremony. But Jōō preferred to display only one item in the alcove. It so happened that Hisamasa and his fellow guest did not agree on the choice, so Jōō, in a diplomatic and original move indicative of his flexibility, displayed both items in the alcove.

Jōō's inventiveness works on two levels. First, he narrowed his selection of items for display to a single work of art—a practice which was to become standard in the later *wabi* style of *chanoyu*. Secondly, he was flexible enough to take his guests' feelings into consideration and adapt his policy accordingly.

Creativity in *chanoyu* cannot be taught; it comes from within the tea master. A pupil of Rikyū once asked the master about the mysteries of the tea ceremony, to which Rikyū replied: "You suggest a feeling of coolness in summer, and coziness in winter; when you burn charcoal you see that the water boils, when you make tea you see that it tastes good. There are no secrets." His pupil seemed unsatisfied with this enigmatic reply since it was obvious that anyone could do this, to which Rikyū replied that if such a man did exist, he would willingly become his pupil.

Tea masters tried to train their pupils to think for themselves, for after they had taught them the procedures of the tea ceremony, the creative part was up to the individual. To help expand the minds of students as part of this personal quest for creativity, Zen inscriptions were chosen to decorate tea rooms, since the Buddhist idea of enlightenment through self-knowledge is said to be the only real way for the student to learn to think independently.

There is another story often told about the tea master Sugiki Fusai and one of his pupils who asked for something to remind him of his teacher's instructions. After some thought Fusai took a piece of burning charcoal from the fire pit, placed it in a small incense brazier, and handed it to his pupil, saying, "I have nothing else to offer you, but take this home and put it in your hearth and keep it burning by performing *chanoyu* morning and evening. If you can keep this up, you will understand all that I have taught you." In other words Fusai's advice was to show his student that he can only learn through his own devices, for only through practice can the novice discover the mysteries of the art.

Another tea master, Joshinsai, based his teachings on the maxim "Conduct the tea ceremony steadily, but modestly, and avoid any behavior that is either showy or affected." He left it to his pupils to find out, through experience, what the best type of conduct was. It is this sense of creativity stemming from Zen philosophy that prevented the tea ceremony from becoming a mundane, merely stylized art.

Invitation to a Tea Ceremony

To the Japanese, the custom of drinking tea is a formal affair with roots that spring from an inherited past that has influenced the habits and manners of the people. To those who are not acquainted with what may seem to be a strange pastime, let us make an imaginary visit to a Japanese home to find out more.

When paying a visit to a close friend it is polite to telephone first and arrange a convenient hour at which to call to give him or her time to make the necessary preparations. Once you are there, you remove your shoes before stepping into the house, and arrange them neatly at the entrance, as is the Japanese custom. For a tea ceremony gathering the footwear is left on the stones outside the guests' entrance. It is considered improper either to wear an overcoat or to carry a handbag when entering a tea room, since this denotes a lack of respect for the host. One leaves all these belongings in the *yoritsuki* (small reception room) in the basket provided.

In the tea room, the seat in front of the alcove is reserved for the guest of honor, and a few articles might be all that the alcove contains. This may seem austere, but it is specially decorated in this fashion, so that each item can receive the proper attention. The same combination of items is never repeated.

When food is served, it will not fill the entire dish, since the container itself is an object of art to be appreciated by the guest. Great pains are taken to ensure that tea articles and food containers are displayed to allow the fullest appreciation of their artistic value. The *kaiseki* meal consists of several dishes brought out one at a time rather than all at once. The host will appreciate comments made on the beauty of the vessels and the flavor of the food. The ingredients of the *kaiseki* food are especially chosen and prepared to suit the season or occasion.

In a *chanoyu* gathering, everything that is seen and used should be an object of appreciation, and this applies not only to precious or famous objects but to everyday utensils as well. This attitude is a reflection of *taru-o-shiru*, meaning "to know what is enough," and it stems from the *wabi* tea style, where beauty is found in the imperfect and the ordinary as well as in the perfect. This attitude permeates the Japanese character; it induces a peacefulness of mind and allows its followers to act calmly and naturally, without conflict.

Tea Architecture and Tea Gardens

All sorts of rooms have been used for tea-drinking: from the splendid *shoin* reception room to the *sōan* (rustic hut). After many changes, it was the *sōan* that finally came to be considered the most appropriate of all places to enjoy tea without distraction.

In all there are four different styles of tea architecture: the large drawing room (*shoin*); the rustic hut-style *kozashiki*, which expressed the merchant's taste; the *sukiya* room, that appealed to the samurai class; and the aristocrat's tea pavilion. It may be felt that only the *sōan* can be considered a true tea room, but it is important to be aware of the background behind the use of each of the four types to understand the evolution of *chanoyu*. Tea gardens are also a reflection of the tea aesthetic, so I will also examine here the origins and features of tea gardens in relation to the tea ceremony.

From *Shoin* to *Sōan*

Prior to the Heian period, most Japanese architecture was in the Shinden style, a style adopted for the building of temples, shrines, and nobles' residences. In the course of time a new samurai-style dwelling was introduced, and later, in the Muromachi period, the *shoin* style was conceived.

The *shoin* was originally a writing room or study usually built as a small wing adjoining the drawing room in a temple. At the height of samurai power it was used as the salon where guests were received. The floor was covered with tatami mats, and the room had an alcove and ornamental shelves.

There were various ways of arranging the alcove and shelves, but the most popular was to have the *shoin* window desk (*tsuke-shoin*) face the veranda, with the alcove and shelves placed side by side next to it. Since there was no artificial lighting available in those days, it was practical for the *shoin* desk to be built near the window, and the alcove to be situated beside it. Even today this is the basic rule followed in designing Japanese-style drawing rooms.

In the early years, six-foot-long (two-meter-long) shelves called *chanoyu-dana*, built in the room adjoining the drawing room, were used for preparing tea. Some of them were built into the wall, while others were smaller in size and portable.

With the *shoin* room the use of the *chanoyu-dana* area for preparing tea was maintained. The room next to the *shoin* was later called *kusari-no-ma* (the chain room). It was so named because it had a fire pit in the floor, over which a kettle was suspended by a chain from the ceiling. Tea was made in this room and then offered to the guests in the reception room.

Some time later when the ritual of making tea came to be performed in the presence of guests, appropriate furniture and vessels were needed for the purpose. Utensil stands similar to ones that had been used in earlier times when tea was performed by the *dōbōshū*, or menservants, and on those occasions when nobles sat on matted platforms to watch *temae* were employed.

The *shoin* were opulent rooms, some as large as eighteen tatami mats (thirty-six square yards / thirty square meters). Because of their size they lacked the atmosphere that would be conducive to proper composure of mind. So it soon became the fashion to close off part of the room with a screen. The resulting space was known as a *kakoi* (enclosure). In later days the *kakoi* played an essential role in the *shoin* tea ceremony, and its design was incorporated into the buildings dedicated only to tea.

In the Muromachi period houses were constructed with pillars set every seven feet (210 centimeters). Tea houses, however, did not follow this rule, with pillars erected every three feet (one meter). This made possible the construction of small houses of four-and-a-half or six mats.

The creation of the *sōan*-style tea house was attributed to the tea master Shukō, who originated the idea of the host personally serving tea. Ceremonies held in large rooms were meant to be observed by people like a performance, while Shukō's tea ceremony was meant to induce intimacy among the host and guests.

The small-scale tea room continued to be constructed until the late Muromachi period. It generally had four-and-a-half mats, whose papered walls and ceiling were similar to those of the *shoin*, but on a much smaller scale. In that room, a *daisu* (utensil stand) was used to allow the host himself to perform *temae*. It is interesting to note that in this transitional period from the *shoin*-room to the smaller, *wabi*-influenced *sōan*-style tea room the *daisu*, a *shoin* room object, was used in this confined space.

According to illustrations of Jōō's style of tea room in the *Record of Yamanoue Sōji*, it was four-and-a-half mats in size and opened onto a garden, facing in a northerly direction. A fire pit was built in the center of the floor. Three sides of the room were walls, while on the northern side there was a paper-covered sliding door adjoining a veranda. The wall on the eastern side separated the tea room from the *shoin*. This kind of tea room was typical of the rooms of that era, and there is written evidence to show that most of the tea practitioners in Sakai imitated this style.

The drawing room of the house was designed with windows to both east and south to admit direct light. By contrast, tea rooms were built to face north, for a more subdued lighting would allow the mind to focus better on the ritual. Probably for the same reason many artists today also build their studios to admit light from the north. The light from this direction is felt to be best for the appreciation of art objects and paintings.

The fire pit used in the tea room was, on average, slightly smaller than one and a half feet square (forty-two centimeters square). In earlier days a charcoal or wood-burning hearth was set in the floor of the living room or the room adjoining the drawing room, but this was never used for guests. It was sometimes as large as a tatami mat. The fire pit in the tea room eventually came to be positioned between host and guests, and the host sat obliquely facing the guests to serve tea.

The fire pit is first constructed out of boards. The inside of the pit is coated with mud, and it is then sunk into the floor by cutting away part of the tatami. A wooden cover is placed over it when it is not in use.

The Characteristics of the *Sōan*-Style Tea House

In the 1570s a great many castles were constructed for and by military generals. Nobunaga's Azuchi Castle was typical of these, its architecture combining elements of a residence and a fortress. Such buildings were large and decorated lavishly to overawe the lord's visitors. The artist Kanō Eitoku (1543–90) and members of his family were commissioned to execute the wall paintings in these castles, as well as of the beautiful paintings and screens found in many of Kyoto's temples. It was during this time that Kanō originated *dami-e*, a technique in which bright colors were painted over a gold background. In describing the effect of such paintings, G. B. Sansom in his book *Japan: A Short Cultural History* says:

> On the walls, mostly of bright gold, there are blue-eyed tigers
> prowling through groves of bamboo, or multi-colored *shishi*—
> mythical beasts like lions, but amiable and curly-haired—that
> gambol among peonies against a golden background. . . . As a
> rule these apartments display, suite after suite, such profusion
> of color and detail, such a deliberate effort to overwhelm the
> eye with splendor, that they come perilously near to vulgarity.
> But from this danger they are generally saved by a certain brav-
> ery, a boldness of stroke and brilliance of design.

In contrast with the samurai, the *machi-shū* of Sakai were wealthy enough to build whatever splendid buildings they chose, but they preferred simplicity. They chose tea rooms without any sort of gaudy decorations that required no artificial elements in their construction, and did not need an abundance of furniture. They influenced changes in the style of the tea rooms and finally invented the simple *sōan*, a rustic hut (called *kozashiki* at the time), using the natural materials of farmhouses: mud, straw, and rough wood. The *sōan* was based on a simple log structure typical of Japanese carpentry, but there was freedom to use any building material that had natural charm. The tea house was built facing south

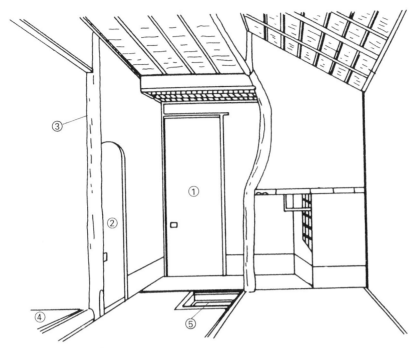

TEA ROOM
This is a *daime*-style tea room in which there are two regular mats for the guests and a shorter mat for the host near the host's door (1). The ceiling (*tenjō*) is set at different heights and angles to add a feeling of space to the small room. As the guest enters the "crawling-through entrance" to the far right (not shown) and raises his head, the first thing he will see is the decorated alcove (4) directly in front of him.

1. Host's entrance (*sadōguchi*).
2. Assistant's entrance (*kyūjiguchi*).
3. Main alcove pillar (*tokobashira*).
4. Alcove (*toko*).
5. Fire pit (*ro*).

instead of north. Excessive light was screened off by constructing deeper eaves. The *sōan* stripped away many of the features of Jōō's style of tea hut, as well as most of the elements of the *shoin*-style structure. Its floor, ceiling, and windows took on new forms that were different from the earlier ones. This type of tea house was conceived to suit the needs of the times, when it was felt that members of all classes should be able to meet in the same room for tea.

Among the various changes in tea architecture brought about by the invention of the *sōan*-style tea house, the following are the most important.

THE FLOOR

Until this period the drawing room always contained a raised platform where higher-ranking people would sit. In the *sōan*, only the floor of the alcove was raised, then it was decorated with thick-tea containers or other tea articles that were highly appreciated among tea masters. By introducing a raised alcove, people from varying backgrounds could share the feeling of sitting together and being treated equally.

THE CEILING

Houses were built with high ceilings, but it was found that height in a small tea room did not make the guests feel more at ease. Even as early as Jōō's time the height of the tea room ceiling was reduced to seven feet

(212 centimeters), and in Rikyū's day to less than six feet (182 centi-meters). But in order to prevent a cramped feeling, sections of the ceiling were staggered at different heights. For example, the alcove ceiling was made a little higher than the ceiling in other parts of the room and was covered with a piece of board, while the ceiling above the host's seat was made a little lower than the section above the guests' place in order to show his humility.

There was also a special ceiling that was formed by the naturally slop-ing roof, called *keshōyaneura tenjō* or *kakekomi tenjō*. This slanting ceiling has the effect of making a room seem larger than it really is.

The lightweight materials used for tea room ceilings, such as shingles, bamboo, and reeds, were quite different from the finely worked boards used for the fretwork ceilings of the large *shoin* rooms.

THE WALLS

Paper walls evolved into mud walls when the builders began to use logs as supporting posts. At first the alcove walls were made of paper, but they too were soon constructed of mud, probably because these warm and softly textured walls were aesthetically in keeping with the dark interior of the tea room.

THE WINDOWS

The windows of the tea room were closely related to the construction of the walls. Before the *sōan* style was invented, a lintel, called a *shiki kamoi*, was placed between one post and the next, and the space between them was made into a window. This conventional method was not suitable for letting light into the small tea hut, and the lintel also looked awkward and out of place. Another type of window, the *shitaji mado*, which was cut into the lower part of the wall, could be built in various sizes and allowed more light in. This design was copied from farmhouse windows that had been built since early times. Such low windows provided a good

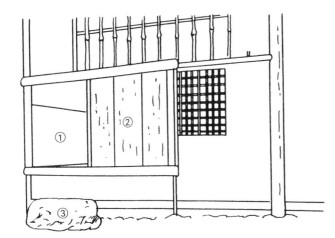

GUESTS' ENTRANCE

Approaching the tea house through the inner garden, the stepping stones lead to the *fumi-ishi*, a high stone (3) for stepping up to the *nijiriguchi*, the guests' entrance. After the door (2) is slid open, the guests crawl through the entrance (1) one at a time, turning around to remove their straw sandals and stand them against the wall of the tea house.

1. Guests' entrance through which a guest has to crawl to enter (*nijiriguchi*).
2. *Nijiriguchi* door slides and is usually made of old timber from the main house.
3. High stone to step up to the *nijiriguchi* (*fumi-ishi*).

flow of air and a better view of the garden or natural scenery when people were seated on the floor.

Another feature of tea hut windows was the use of bamboo grilles, which not only let more light in, but helped to create a mood conducive to serenity of mind.

THE HOST'S ENTRANCE (*Sadōguchi*)

This is a small entrance, originally lower than the height of the average Japanese, a device that forced the host to bow his head to enter and instilled a sense of humility.

THE GUESTS' ENTRANCE (*Nijiriguchi*)

This is the entrance to the tea room through which guests have to crouch. It is said that in Jōō's time one had to enter the tea room on hands and knees from the veranda. An old illustration still in existence shows this entrance with a half-rolled bamboo screen outside its paper-covered door, but today the entrance is made of wood.

The guests' low entrance signified humility, but another reason for creating the low entrance was to make the guests feel they were entering a different world. Lowering the head during entry was also taken as a sign of respect to the other guests already seated in the room.

When the *sōan* first came into use, its entrance was so low that one had to stoop very low while crawling into the room. It is said that old storm doors from the main house were used in the earliest *sōan* tea houses as the sliding door for the *nijiriguchi*. This is evident from the position of its *san* (crosspiece). Later the door of the *nijiriguchi* was made of three boards: two old pieces of timber and a narrower new piece to finish the door.

Some say that this came about because the *sōan* was originally supposed to be built from the old timbers of the main house, so that all kinds of wood would have been used in its construction. Thus both old and new wood was always used in the *nijiriguchi* door to symbolize the fact that the house was made of discarded timber. Whatever the origin of the idea, it makes a pleasing contrast to have a piece of high-quality grained timber combined with old timber.

Some people also say that the *nijiriguchi* is designed in such a way as to prevent the entrance of intruders, but this is doubtful because the door is only a quarter of an inch (0.6 centimeters) thick and can easily be broken with a push. The bamboo grilles are fixed only with nails, so that they are easily replaceable every year. The windows themselves are fragile in structure, covered only by a sliding paper-covered screen, and the wall surrounding them is not much more than an inch (2.5 centimeters) thick.

The host takes off the *nijiriguchi* door in order to wash and wipe it before the guests arrive. When the guest crouches on the stepping stone and touches the door, he finds it still wet in places, which gives a feeling of freshness. The door is left slightly ajar, so that the guest can open it with ease. The moment he opens it, the alcove and hanging scroll come into view. From this vantage point, he can see the interior of the small room. After a quick glimpse, he bends over and creeps in, head first. As a result of his difficult entry, he is made more conscious of the fact that he is in a special place.

The last guest to enter shuts and latches the door. This door latch is made so simply that it does not guard the room against danger, but it gives the guests a feeling of isolation. Perhaps the purpose of building the *nijiriguchi* is to make those who pass through it realize that they are entering another world.

The other features in the tea room—pillars, lintels, frames, ledges—look
very light and fragile. Much care is taken to ensure an aesthetic balance
between their height and width. The *akari shōji*, a sliding paper-covered
screen with a wooden frame and lattice, is used for letting in light as well
as protecting guests from the cold wind. Translucent white paper of
varying widths is pasted on the frame, and in tea rooms, thin seams
where the paper joins are made to appear between the lattices.

In Rikyū's time there was a discussion about the proper width of the
seam. When Rikyū was asked about this, he said: "One *bu* (one-eighth of
an inch / three millimeters) is too narrow, but one-and-a-half *bu* is too
wide." This answer did not provide an exact measure, but by defining the
maximum and the minimum, Rikyū indicated that the width had to be
decided according to the size of the room. This episode shows how
precise Rikyū was, even when it came to such minor details.

The introduction of the *sōan* brought about various changes in the way
tea was served and the tea utensils were used. Up to that time, a large utensil stand had been used in a four-and-a-half-mat tea room, but because
the *sōan* was too small to accommodate one, this had to be eliminated.
As a result, people were freed from former restrictions on the way that
tea articles were used, and this in turn helped make tea more accessible.

Changes in the Tea Room

In Matsuya Hisamasa's *Record of Tea Ceremonies*, he stated that he renovated his tea hut many times. Hisamasa, who lived in Nara, often visited
Sakai, which was the center of the tea ceremony in his day, and he
seemed to be influenced by the tea hut fashions of Sakai. Following the
appearance of the four-and-a-half-mat tea hut, other types with four
mats, three mats, and two mats were devised. Tea huts were all constructed on one-mat or half-mat units, which meant that the rooms were
either square or rectangular in shape, and lacked variation.

Later on, the *daime* tatami was devised, which was about one foot five inches (forty-five centimeters) shorter than the regular mat, for with the disappearance of the large utensil stand, less space was required. With the advent of this new type of tatami, a new shape of room was developed, with a new style of ceiling. This was called a *daime*-type room.

At the same time, the fire pit was placed between the host and guests, and the *nakabashira* (central post) was built close to it. An extended wall (*sode kabe*) was attached to the post, and a shelf was fixed to its side. This post also played a decorative role, and straight as well as curved specimens were used to attract the eye.

These variations were all developed during Rikyū's lifetime. After his death, daimyo-style tea practioners such as Furuta Oribe and Kobori Enshū also exerted their influence on the design of the tea room. They changed the *sōan* into a more refined room to suit the warrior tastes and, most notably, altered the use of light in the tea hut. Oribe preferred a bright space over the dimness that Rikyū had felt would soothe the mind. One of the most famous of Enshū's tea houses is the Bosen room in Koho-an, a temple within the compounds of Daitoku-ji in Kyoto. In this room the evening sunlight reflects off the ceiling into the alcove, a well-calculated effect that illuminates any hanging scroll set in a flattering manner.

The way that guests were treated also underwent some changes under the daimyo tea masters. Oribe's tea room had a *shōbanseki* (seat for minor guests), which was a one-mat area situated behind a paper screen outside the tea room. Nobles and their attendants were to sit separately, and a new etiquette was introduced to segregate the ranks. An entrance combining the host's entrance and the nobles' entrance was constructed, and the earlier principle of social equality in the tea room disappeared.

In the Edo period, the convention of placing the alcove where it could be best viewed by the principle guest underwent some modification. Various combinations were created. The word *gezadoko*, literally the

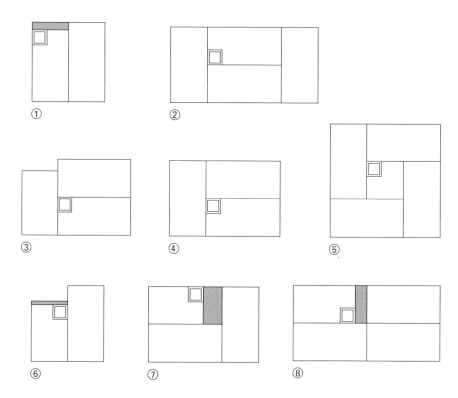

EIGHT VARIATIONS OF THE TEA ROOM (LAYOUTS 3 AND 6 ARE *DAIME*)

1. Two-mat room with fire pit built into the host's mat and a 3-inch (7.5-centimeter) board behind it (*nijō*).
2. Rectangular four-mat room with the fire pit between host and guests (*naga yojō*).
3. *Daime*-style room with two guest mats plus a shorter mat for the host; fire pit is between the host and guests (*nijō daime*).
4. Three-mat room with fire pit between host and guests (*hira sanjō*).
5. Four-and-a-half-mat room with fire pit between host and guests (*yojōhan*).
6. *Daime* style with one guest mat and one short mat for host; the fire pit is built into the host's mat between host and guests (*ichijō daime*).
7. Three-mat room with fire pit built into host's mat on the wall side and with a 18-inch (45-centimeter) board (*fuka-sanjō*).
8. Old-style rectangular four-mat room with the fire pit between host and guests, but with a 6-inch (15-centimeter) board (*naga yojō*).

alcove placed in a lesser position, indicates this change. In the style called *teishudoko*, the host made tea in front of this alcove. The Jiko-in tea room built by Katagiri Seishu in Yamato, Nara Prefecture, is representative of this style. Exemplary of the *gezadoko* style is the Jo-an tea room in

Inuyama, Aichi Prefecture, constructed by Oda Uraku and designated a
national treasure in 1951.

Enshū devised the arrangement whereby the host's seat and the
alcove were placed side by side, like a stage. Such an arrangement suited
tea ceremonies performed by Enshū himself.

The *sōan* was a tea hut with none of the *shoin*-style elements included
in its design, but some of these were reintroduced by Enshū and gradually the tea hut developed into a *shoin*-style tea room so that it would
better serve as a reception room for visiting nobility. The *shoin* was often
constructed next to the drawing room so that it would be easily accessible to guests, while the *sōan* was separated from the main building.

The *shoin*-style tea room, like the proper *shoin* room, had paper walls
and a transom with openwork (*ranma*), and its sliding door frames were
coated with black lacquer. Ornamental shelves and a *shoin* desk were
added. In the Edo period, the word *shoin* was applied mainly to the
drawing room. Tea rooms in a daimyo or court noble's residence were
called *sukiya* (room for *suki*) since from the latter half of the Muromachi
period the word *suki* was used interchangeably for the tea ceremony. The
term continued to prevail in the Edo period even though *shoin*-style
architecture and *sōan*-style tea huts, often boasting *daime* (small-sized)
tatami and *nakabashira* (central post), were utilized. Today, the word
sukiya refers to tea rooms and general structures built in a traditional
Japanese fashion.

Sōtan was a noted tea master during this period, but unlike Rikyū, he
did not give instruction to warriors and clung tenaciously to the *wabi* tea
style. He preserved the formalities of the Rikyū tea room, and his style
became the model for the students of the Senke school of tea.

Kanamori Sōwa was a tea master descended from samurai stock, and
had access to court nobles, whom he guided in both the tea ceremony
and tea architecture. He had a strong influence on the design of temples
and nobles' residences, and he preferred the restfulness of a small tea

room. In contrast with Sōtan's tastes, Sōwa wished to impart a sense of elegance to the tea ceremony.

Thus *wabi* and the daimyo styles of tea coexisted to a certain extent from the time that Hideyoshi served tea at the Imperial Palace with Rikyū as his *sadō* in 1585. This was the event that established the form of the aristocratic tea ceremony, with Rikyū's *wabi* style as its basis.

Prince Toshihito (1579–1629), a member of the first generation of the Katsuranomiya family, constructed tea houses on the grounds of his palace in 1602. Later, he began work on the Katsura Imperial Villa, which was completed by his son, Prince Toshitada (1619–62). This villa represents a prime example of the *sukiya* style and contains *shoin* drawing rooms that incorporate elements from the *sōan*-style tea hut. The former emperor Go-mizunoo (1596–1680), who was well-versed in the tea ceremony, also built such tea rooms in his palace and at some temples.

What most distinguishes these tea buildings from the pure *sōan*-style hut is the aristocratic refinement of taste. This can be seen in the exquisitely shaped door pulls on the sliding doors, the artistic designs of the lower wood panels of the *shōji* (paper-covered screens) and the elaborate arrangement of shelves. The pine, bamboo, and plum designs that decorate the host's entrance to the Tōshin-tei tea room at the Minase Shrine in Osaka are fine examples of this aristocratic taste.

Simultaneously, there was a trend among commoners to make the structure of the *sōan* more intricate. This influence can be seen in the *ita-datami* (a board that was added to the tea room in order to enlarge the space), or in the idea of designing the alcove on a smaller scale. Most people sought to display their originality in minor details, while at the same time it became the fashion to use expensive timber to make the house more splendid. Thus the conventional, simple tea house that had symbolized the spirit of tea gradually came to acquire more decorative elements.

In the Meiji period, when Western-style architecture was introduced into Japan, a blend of Japanese and European styles was frequently adopted for homes, and purely Japanese buildings became scarce. In keeping with this tendency, orthodox tea houses and elegant tea huts disappeared, and the only buildings being built that resembled tea houses were those set in the grounds of restaurants and inns.

Tea Houses of Today

In early times, the *sōan* was generally made from natural materials found nearby or from the old timbers of the main house. Through studying old tea structures that have been preserved, we can see that they were usually built of several kinds of timber, while in residential homes only one kind of wood (Japanese cypress or Japanese cedar) was used.

Tea houses built today follow the older designs in the choice of materials. However, it is now difficult to obtain materials that used to be available in earlier times, and there are few carpenters who are able to build these tea houses, for the art of using plain logs for pillars and beams and making mud walls has become highly specialized.

In early times tea houses could easily be renovated according to the taste of the time, but today it is too expensive to change a structure once it has been built. This may also be due to present methods of construction. One of the basic characteristics of early tea architecture was the lightness of the structure. It was unnecessary to lay a foundation, as was the case with residential homes. Instead, tea house pillars were set on stones about eight inches in diameter. But now the beams and eaves of the tea house have become larger and heavier, since they are constructed by modern methods. They also require firm foundations of concrete, and the result is a permanent, solid, heavy appearance. They can hardly be called *sōan* in the true sense of the word.

Recently, even prefabricated tea houses have been put on the market, and, although they offer everyone the opportunity to own a tea house, it creates the temptation to standardize the style. The tea house should be designed not only in accordance with the size of its garden, but also to take into account the way its roof looks from the main house. In a similar manner, windows are designed on the basis of the amount and quality of light they admit, as well as the view they command. The modern tea house today lacks the warmth, softness, and comfort of the individually designed tea hut, and unfortunately the art and skill of earlier artisans are rarely found today. Houses styled naturally and without artifice differ greatly from those produced through modern techniques of imitation.

The Origin of Tea Gardens

The garden surrounding a tea house differs from one outside a drawing room: while the latter may be viewed from a seated position within the house, the tea house garden is designed so the viewer may enjoy the scenery as he walks along its paths.

According to the records of tea gatherings during the Muromachi period, the garden played an important part in tea entertainment, for after a banquet the guests went out to the garden to rest in the cool air near the pond, and only after that went into a pavilion to have tea. A quiet place in the garden away from the main house was felt to be most suitable for drinking tea, and the participants felt more relaxed after going into the garden for a walk. One tea pavilion of this type that is still in existence today is the Kinkaku of Rokuonji temple in Kyoto.

An illustration of Jōō's garden around his four-and-a-half-mat tea hut, found in the *Record of Yamanoue Sōji*, shows two gardens, the *waki-no-tsubonouchi* (outer section close to the garden entrance) and the *omote-tsubonouchi* (the inner section near the tea hut).

Another illustration of a Jōō garden for the same type of tea hut describes the *omote-tsubonouchi* as the *niwa* (garden) and the *waki-no-tsub-onouchi* as the inner garden. It is apparent from these terms that there was some difference in function between the outer garden and the inner garden, the latter being merely a passageway leading to the tea hut. The same picture shows that the inner garden had an entrance from which a five-foot- (152-centimeter-) long path led to the veranda adjoining the reception room.

A tea book written at the time, *Senrin*, stated that the garden in front of a four-and-a-half-mat tea hut should not contain any plants or stones, lest the guests be distracted by the view, although it was permissible to have some greenery around the stone washbasin. It seems that this prohibition lasted for some time; a plan of the tea hut built by Matsuya Hisamasa shows that the garden was laid out very simply, devoid of any plants, except for some moss and one maple tree.

Although Jōō's garden contained no trees, it undoubtedly had a lovely atmosphere. A book written at the time states that pines of various shapes could be seen overhanging the fence of his garden and provided a fine view in contrast to the starkness of the garden itself.

When all four sides of the tea house were walled and the door of the guests' entrance was constructed of wood, there was no fear that people would be distracted by the outside view. Then, the garden design might encompass trees, shrubs, and stepping stones enabling the guests to walk around the garden with ease.

The forerunner of the *roji* (the present-day name for the tea garden) came into existence as a place of quiet in the city where people could enter a different world in spite of being just a short distance from the city's hustle and bustle.

The original word *roji* meant a passageway leading to a tea hut. In the Edo period, characters signifying "dewy path" were applied to the name *roji*, and a spiritual connotation was added to its meaning.

Tea gardens were also designed to provide an outside entrance to the tea house, instead of entering the drawing room of a home through the front door and having to walk through a corridor or adjoining room to get to the tea room. With a garden entrance, one could enter the tea house directly without disturbing the household.

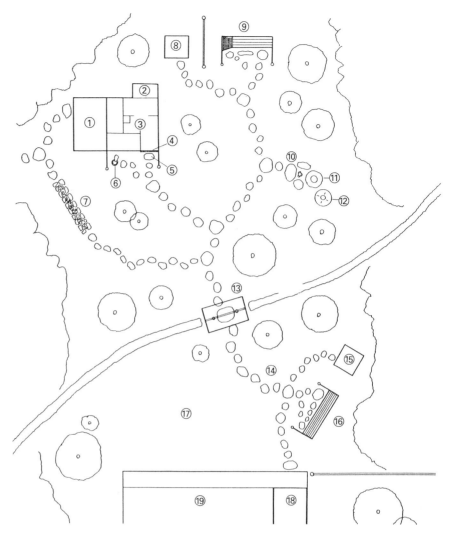

LAYOUT OF A TEA GARDEN

1. Host's preparation room (*mizuya*).
2. Alcove (*toko*).
3. Tea room (*chashitsu*).
4. Guest's entrance (*nijiriguchi*).
5. High stone at entrance to tea room (*fumi-ishi*).
6. Debris pit (*chiri-ana*).
7. Paved stone path (*nobedan*).
8. Toilet (*setchin*).
9. Inner waiting arbor (*uchi-koshikake*).
10. Washbasin area (*tsukubai*).
11. Stone washbasin (*chōzubachi*).
12. Stone lantern (*ishi-dōrō*).
13. Middle gate (*chūmon*).
14. Stepping stones (*tobi-ishi*).
15. Toilet (*setchin*).
16. Outer waiting arbor (*soto-koshikake*).
17. Main garden of the house.
18. The room where guests arrive first to prepare themselves for the start of the gathering (*yoritsuki*).
19. House proper.

According to the *Record of Yamanoue Sōji*, a veranda (*en*) was added to the four-and-a-half–mat tea hut; the guests would pass through the tea garden and mount the *en* before entering the tea house. Tea houses less than three-mat had no veranda.

As the years passed, tea gardens became larger. The first gardens were built by townspeople who had little land to spare for a tea garden, but when the tea ceremony was adopted by the samurai and nobles, there was more land available around their castles and palaces, and so the scale of tea gardens grew. New styles were then adopted, including the double *roji*, in which a second garden was built outside the one surrounding the tea house, the two separated by a bamboo fence; or the triple *roji*, in which a third garden was added around the other two.

A number of arbors were built in these gardens, such as a *yoritsuki* (a place near the garden gate where the guests assembled and changed into fresh socks before the entertainment), and a *soto-machiai* (an arbor outside the *roji* where guests waited for their host). There were also other elements incorporated through the centuries, which I will mention briefly.

STEPPING STONES

Over the years differing scales were used in the arrangement of stepping stones. Those laid out under Rikyū's direction were large and meant to afford easy walking. Rikyū's method was a manifestation of his maxim that there should be: "A ratio of six for *watari* and four for *kei*." *Watari* means practicality, and *kei*, appearance, or artistic balance. Rikyū put more stress on practicality, while Oribe held "four for *watari* and six for *kei*" as the ideal aesthetic proportion.

The difference between the two methods may be seen in two distinct garden arrangements. In the Myōki-an tea house designed by Rikyū, the stepping stones were arranged in a natural order, whereas those in front of the middle *shoin* of the Katsura Imperial Villa, said to have been laid out under the guidance of a tea master of the Oribe school, were arranged very differently.

Gradually the design of stepping stones came to follow established patterns. They differed according to which stones of what size were placed where, taking into consideration their artistic balance. At first mountain rocks were used, but later stones from the river and sea were included,

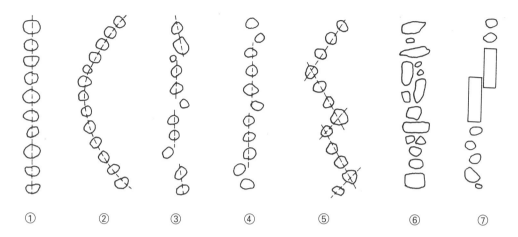

DIFFERENT CONFIGURATIONS OF STEPPING STONES

1. Straight line (*choku-uchi*).
2. Broad curve (*ō-magari*).
3. Chain of pairs linked with extras (*niren-uchi*).
4. Chain of threes linked with extras strewn (*sanren-uchi*).
5. Geese in flight (*gan-uchi*).
6. "Seven-five-three" (*shichigosan-uchi*).
7. Rafts (*ikada-uchi*).

RIKYU STYLE
Simple, small, and set almost flush with the ground.

ORIBE STYLE
Geometrically arranged stepping stones.

PAVED STONE PATHS

1. Checkerboard (*ichimatsu-jiki*).   4. Cracked ice (*hyōmon-jiki*).
2. Diamond (*shihan-jiki*).   5. Hailstones (*ō-arare-jiki*).
3. Tortoise carapace (*kikkō-jiki*). 6. Jumble (*yose-ishi-jiki*).

and rare and curiously formed stones became especially valued.

In *wabi* gardens, natural stones of medium size were sunk into the earth, but the stones in the paths of daimyo-style tea gardens were slightly raised. Large stones were placed at long intervals for the path through the outer *roji*, and small stones were placed at short intervals for the path through the inner *roji*.

PLANTS

The *roji* was planted with trees in a way that would suggest the atmosphere of a remote mountain. Trees such as pine, cedar, and oak were selected, and shrubs and grass were planted around them. Flowering trees were avoided on purpose, for it was said that if one's eye were distracted by the *roji*, one's mind might be distracted from the mood of the tea ceremony. If one saw flowers growing in the garden, then those arranged so carefully in the tea room might fail to hold charm by comparison. Over the years more rules were added. One of them was to avoid the use of plants that were fragrant, poisonous, or thorny.

MOSS

In early times, river sand or white sand was said to be an element of the tea garden. Later, moss or low bamboo bushes were planted as ground covering to evoke inpages of scenery. Today pine needles are spread over moss in winter to protect it from the frost, but they are not used ornamentally.

The soil in the vicinity of Kyoto is especially suited to the growth of moss. Since it is granitic in composition, it drains well and always contains some moisture, which is necessary for raising moss. Among the many kinds of moss, the *sugi-goke* variety, which resembles a miniature tree and grows in foggy areas, is especially highly prized. This moss has a beauty distinct from most other varieties, and is often cultivated in tea gardens.

THE MIDDLE GATE (*Chūmon*)
The middle gate is meant to cut off the outer world from the inner realm of tea. Some tea gardens have two gates: an outer gate at the street entrance that enables the guest to go to the *machiai* without passing through the main entrance of the domestic building, and a middle gate to separate the inner and outer gardens. It is at the middle gate where the host greets his guests for the first time, silently, with a bow.

At first the middle gate was a simple wooden structure, but later, one with earthen walls and a small entrance came to be used. A hedge was grown beside the gate and also surrounded the garden.

THE WASHBASIN (*Tsukubai*)
One noteworthy element in the inner garden was a stone washbasin where guests rinsed their mouths and washed their hands as an act of purification before entering the tea room. Originally a standing washbasin was placed at the end of the veranda that adjoined the reception room so that it could be used without stepping into the garden. The basin was large and tall, in keeping with the noble's custom of having his servant pour water for him with a ladle when he wished to wash his hands. After it was placed in the *roji*, however, it became shorter and smaller, so that guests had to squat by its side to wash their hands by themselves. *Tsukubai* literally means "squatting."

Another reason for the use of a smaller basin and the shorter *tsukubai* is that the *sōan* tea ceremony required the host, before receiving his guests, to bring a pail of water with which to fill the washbasin. In other

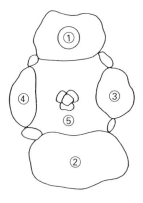

TSUKUBAI
1. Stone washbasin (*chōzubachi*).
2. Long flat stone for guest to stand on while washing hands (*mae-ishi*).
3. Stone for placing hot water bucket on (*yuoke-ishi*).
4. Stone for placing lamp on (*teshoku-ishi*).
5. Drainage pebbles around the base of the water basin (*gorota-ishi*).

styles of washbasins a bamboo pipe would constantly refill the basin with water from a nearby lake or stream, but in the *sōan* style, it is the host's function to provide water.

Before long, there developed a prescribed arrangement for the stones near the *tsukubai*. On its right side is a flat stone, *yuoke-ishi*, where, in winter, a vessel of hot water is placed for the comfort of elderly guests. To the left, a high stone called *teshoku-ishi* (lamp stone) is placed. This stone is used for placing a candle on in dawn tea ceremonies or ones performed after dark. Sometimes the positions of the stones are reversed. While the inside of the basin is kept clean through constant care, the outside and the stones surrounding it are left covered by moss.

There is a special drainage system devised for the washbasin, where a long flat stone, called *mae-ishi*, is placed for the guests to kneel or crouch on while washing. Between this stone and the basin is the *suimon* (water gate), an indentation in the ground filled with pebbles or broken tile, which catches the overflow from the basin in the washing process, and through which the water reaches a drainpipe underneath. The pebbles (*gorota-ishi*) in this hole are kept clean by constant hand polishing, and are arranged with great care.

THE STONE LANTERN (*Ishi-dōrō*)
Lanterns were introduced to Japan from China and Korea through Buddhism, and were first used in Buddhist temples. Only later were they employed at Shinto shrines. According to written evidence, they were also used in ordinary gardens during the Muromachi period.

A stone lantern was used for lighting the inner tea garden, and was generally placed by the side of the washbasin, while other smaller lanterns were also placed here and there in the garden. Sometimes only the lantern without the base was placed on the stone beside the washbasin. Great care was taken in the exact positioning of the stone lantern by the washbasin and the direction in which it faced. According to the

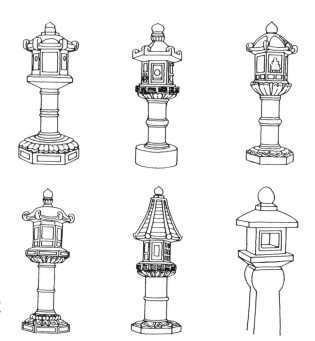

ISHI-DŌRŌ

Stone lanterns used in a tea garden, often styled after famous temple lanterns.

eleven-volume *Kaiki*, written in 1724, the light should fall on the basin.

In the daytime the paper door of the lantern is lifted and the inside cleaned. At night an oil lamp is put into the lantern, shielded from the wind by the paper-covered door. Various ideas were employed to provide more aesthetic effects; for example, on moonlit nights more wicks were added, while in snowy weather the light was not used at all. Thus stone lanterns are not merely garden ornaments or a means of illumination, but their beauty when lit should inspire the admiration of the beholder.

THE AREA AROUND THE GUESTS' ENTRANCE

A stone higher than the other stones, called *fumi-ishi*, is placed in front of the guests' entrance. It is just high enough to enable the crouching guest's hand to naturally reach the entrance, and its surface is just wide enough for one pair of feet. Since it is placed before such an important place, it is a carefully chosen stone, oblong and wider at the bottom than the top, and with features distinguishing it from other stones.

Another stone, placed a little lower than the *fumi-ishi*, is called *otoshi-ishi*, and in front of it another stone, *nori-ishi*, is placed. These three stones are arranged precisely so that the *nori-ishi* can be used to catch raindrops from the eaves of the tea house.

From this area in front of the guests' entrance, the garden path divides into two, one going in the direction of the *chiri-ana* (a pit into which fallen leaves are placed), and the other toward the *katanakake* (the

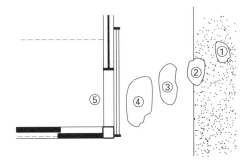

shelf where a samurai's swords were placed before entering the tea house). Stones of various shapes and sizes are arranged along both paths and pebbles scattered around them.

THE PIT FOR DEBRIS (*Chiri-ana*)

The garden is always kept clean, but falling leaves from the trees or shrubs inevitably litter the garden after it has been swept. The leaves are picked up with special green bamboo chopsticks and dropped into a device called a *chiri-ana*. Originally the *chiri-ana* was positioned out of sight, but later it came to be part of the area viewed by guests. Historical records say that a flower-decorated *chiri-ana* was seen in the Azuchi-Momoyama period, but later *chiri-ana* contained an additional stone for ornamental purposes.

The size of the *chiri-ana* varies in relation to the size of the tea house. The larger size is square, and the smaller type circular. The above-mentioned green bamboo chopsticks are laid symbolically inside it, and a few twigs with leaves from the garden are put in for effect.

THE DISTINGUISHED GUEST'S ENTRANCE (*Kininguchi*)

Besides the *nijiriguchi*, some tea houses have another entrance for the reception of distinguished guests. Such an entrance is covered with paper sliding doors and serves a secondary purpose of letting in more light. The stepping stone in front of it is higher and longer than the one used for other guests. Until the Azuchi-Momoyama period the tea house had either a *nijiriguchi* or a *kininguchi*, but never both. Later, some tea houses started to employ both.

The debris pit is seen in the foreground of the guest's entrance, with a twig from the garden and bamboo chopsticks.

STONE PAVEMENTS (*Nobedan*)

This is another path through the garden, distinguished in its appearance by an alternation of oblong and small natural stones. The contrast between the artificially cut stones and the natural stones gives an interesting effect to the path; a noteworthy example is the famous Shin-no-tobi-ishi path of the Katsura Imperial Villa.

THE WAITING ARBOR (*Machiai*)

In the ordinary course of the tea ceremony, the guests wait for the host on two occasions in the garden. The first time is before entering the tea house, when the host appears and bows to the guests in the outer garden. The second occurrence takes place after the short recess (*nakadachi*) before reentering the tea hut. Two separate waiting arbors with benches accommodate the guests. Stones are placed before the bench for resting the feet. The stone for the principal guest is different from the others, either a little larger or placed higher and slightly apart from the others. In some arbors one long stone is used for all the other guests.

WATERING THE GARDEN

One of the rules of the tea ceremony is that the garden should be kept fresh and green through frequent sprinkling. This is done to enhance its beauty. Great care is taken in the manner of watering, which is referred to in Japanese by the expression to "strike" with water to purposely create a feeling of freshness and purity, rather than to sprinkle. Generally, lower portions of fences, walls, and gates are watered. Even after rain, the lower portion of the gate and the wooden walls are watered. This practice tells the guests that the host's preparations for the tea ceremony are complete. If one arrives at a *chanoyu* gathering to find that the garden has not been sprinkled, it is a sign that the host is not yet ready.

There are actually three fixed patterns of watering the garden during the course of a tea entertainment, which are collectively known as *sanro*. The first sprinkling is carried out before the guests enter the tea room, the second, in the short recess between the first and second parts of the tea ceremony, and the third before the guests leave.

Thus far I have related some of the changes that have been made to the tea garden over the years, noteworthy features of the tea garden, and its care. The tea garden, like the tea house, is divided into four types, and varies according to the taste and social status of the owner. At the same time, it must also be in harmony with the tea house: a plain garden suits a simple hut, and an elaborate landscape garden goes with a grand tea house.

The outer garden of the Dai Nihon Chadō Gakkai tea rooms. A paved walkway takes the guest around a corner and to the inner garden.

The stepping stones lead to the middle gate at the far left (partially obscured by foliage) and then to the four-and-a-half-mat Santoku-an tea house in the rear.

A stone water basin sits in front of the Chisui-tei tea hut on the grounds of the Dai Nihon Chadō Gakkai in Tokyo. The basin was originally owned by the Matsura clan, a daimyo family in Kyushu. The sound of trickling water can be heard continuously from the tea room.

The inner garden of Chisui-tei has a powerful configuration of stepping stones and a natural balance between tall trees and shrubbery.

The waiting arbor for guests at the Santoku-an tea house. The stones that mark the seating positions are each a different size and shape, the largest one indicating the seat of the main guest.

A bound stone signals that the path is not to be used on the present occasion.

The guests' entrance to the one-mat *daime*-style Chisui-tei tea hut. Of the stepping stones leading to the tea room, the second-to-last stone is higher than the preceding ones to protect the guests' kimono from the gutter that catches rain run off from the roof. ▶

OVERLEAF

The interior of the Chisui-tei tea house relies on many types of natural wood. A tree trunk, with its natural curves and contortions intact, marks the edge of the board that adjoins the short *daime* mat. To the right is the guests' door, made from old timbers.

III

THE
CEREMONY

Temae

The Origin and Meaning of *Temae*

Social evenings during the Heian period of the ninth century were high-lighted by popular games devised by the nobility for their own amusement, including the competition of incense-smelling mentioned earlier, and *monoawase*, a simple card game involving the pairing off of pictures of different kinds of shells, insects, flowers, or grasses. As social activity increased, the nature of these games became more complex and special rules and procedures were devised for them.

In the same way the tea ceremony also became more complex as new rules were invented to enhance these social gatherings, and gradually the nature of *chanoyu* changed. The first major change was a proliferation of Japanese-made tea utensils. Previously, most had been imported from China. New procedures were also devised for indoor ceremonies and those conducted outdoors on the lawn. Many new kinds of tea articles were added.

Some of the reasons for the changes in *temae* over the centuries were historical and sociological. Different social classes infused their own customs and traditions into *temae*. And during the Edo period, when the *iemoto* system was introduced for all the professions, schools began passing on their individual techniques to students, and the types of *temae* increased.

Temae is the procedure used for making and serving tea. It is memorized in much the same way as learning the steps of a dance. When *temae* is performed before large audiences and the host becomes the center of attention, the real meaning of the action is lost in the spectacle. It is not, as is commonly believed, the means and end of the tea ceremony. *Temae* has a deeper and more subtle aspect that is only apparent when it is properly performed.

The origins of *temae* can be found in the actions of the *dōbōshū*, the lord's attendant whose duty was to handle valuable utensils carefully and to serve tea in a graceful manner. In the course of time, small tea gatherings where the host himself made the tea among commoners became popular in Sakai. The host's movements while making tea became an important aspect of the event and served to entertain his guests. The specific name *temae* was given to this performance.

The origin of *temae* has been attributed to Shukō. He said that by concentrating the mind on the gestures as a meditative exercise, *temae* acquired a deep spiritual meaning for the student. Shukō also taught his students how to behave inconspicuously and unaffectedly, and these ideas became the essence of *temae*. Gradually, as the ceremony became less complex, the rules of *temae* were simplified.

There are three basic elements present in the concept of *temae*: arrangement, purification, and calmness of mind. Arrangement refers to the carrying of the utensils into the tea room and setting them down properly. When the utensils are brought into the room one by one, they can be admired individually from close proximity, and they are so arranged that their beauty can be admired from many different angles. The element of surprise would be lessened if they were brought in all at once.

Purification is the act of cleaning the tea bowl, tea container, and tea scoop. Warming the bowl with hot water and wiping it is nothing more than a standard cleaning preparation, but the custom of passing a folded silk cloth called a *fukusa* over the tea caddy and scoop is a formality that has been handed down from the *dōbōshū*. The cleaning of the tea caddy with a *fukusa* symbolizes a cleansing and purification of the mind, and if done without pretension it induces a feeling of peace and tranquility in the guests.

This calmness of feeling can be disrupted if the tea master is too quick in his actions or too hurried in his pace. After the cakes have been served, a short period of time is given over to allow the guests an opportunity to admire the hanging scroll and the vase of flowers. Then the tea is made and served to the guests, who drink it and pass the bowl back to the host. He then rinses it and begins to put all the articles away efficiently but

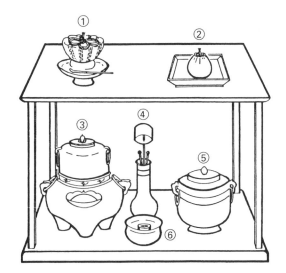

DAISU

Shin-no-shin daisu (the most formal of the formal styles of utensil stand arrangement)

1. Tea bowl in a silk drawstring pouch on a lacquered stand, with the tea scoop. 2. Small square lacquered tray on which is placed the tea container in its own silk drawstring pouch. 3. Iron kettle on a bronze brazier. 4. Ladle stand containing ladle and ornamental metal chopsticks. 5. Bronze cold water container. 6. Waste-water receptacle in front containing the ladle rest.

without hurry. The *temae* comes to an end, having lasted some twelve or thirteen minutes in all, leaving the guests with a feeling of contentment and satisfaction at having partaken in a tranquil ritual.

Different Types of *Temae*

Temae can be divided into three main types: the *shoin* style, the *sōan* style, and the *hiroma* style.

The *shoin*-style *temae* makes use of a utensil stand called a *daisu*, which has an upper and lower shelf on which all the utensils used for the tea ceremony are placed. The host conducts the preparations with utmost solemnity and in strict accordance with the rules of etiquette. It is also stated that his mind should be free of all mundane thoughts while he is performing the ceremony. Although there are more than sixty variations of the *shoin*-style *temae*, the three principal ones are known as *shin*, *gyō* and *sō*.

The *sōan* style differs from the above in its conception of the host's duty, which is to serve his guests in a less formal and more personal way. The host and his guests sit facing one another across the fire pit, or *ro*, and the tea is drunk from rustic utensils that are used in the *wabi* style of tea ceremony. Only the tea container, cold water jar, and brazier and kettle are placed in the room beforehand, and the host himself brings out the other utensils one by one as the ceremony progresses. This procedure is known as *hakobidate*, and distinguishes the *sōan* from the *shoin* style.

The *hiroma*, or large room, style evolved during the Edo period and is by far the most regulated of the three types and most suited for very large gatherings of people. The design of the room is different: the alcove is decorated in a special way, and shelves are built into the room to hold all the utensils. The host brings in two tea bowls at the same time and prepares tea in them one after the other. This is known as *kasane jawan*.

SŌAN

A *sōan*-style tea room with one mat for the guests and a *daime* mat for the host.

HIROMA

A large *hiroma*-style tea room with shelves adjoining the alcove.

Some other styles include the *kinindate*, which is related to the *hiroma* style except that it is only performed for exalted individuals; the *chasen-kazari*, where specific utensils receive special attention; the *shomō mono*, where the host asks the principal guest to arrange the flowers in the alcove; and the *shichijishiki temae*, where several people take turns in acting as hosts and guests, according to a draw from a box called *orisue*. This style of *temae* is performed in silence, since its chief purpose is unison of action. In addition, there is a style where host and guests are seated on chairs (*ryūrei*), another only performed outdoors (*nodate*), and one where all the utensils are placed in a box (*chabako*).

The Order of *Temae*
Despite the many different types of *temae* that have been devised, the basic rules are common to all.

ARRANGEMENT OF UTENSILS
Tea utensils must be arranged in a way that facilitates their removal and replacement. Depending on the type of *temae*, when some utensils are taken out for use and others left for decoration, great care must go into the planning and arrangement so that everything proceeds smoothly during the performance.

WIPING THE UTENSILS
The cleaning of the tea container and the tea scoop (*chashaku*) is an important act, for it signifies a spiritual cleansing of the mind and heart, during which all thoughts pertaining to the temporal world should be dismissed. When making *koicha* or thick tea, the ceramic tea container is wiped first with a folded silk cloth called a *fukusa*. Similarly in the preparation of *usucha*, thin tea, it is the lacquered tea container that is wiped first.

CHASEN
Tea whisks.

WARMING THE TEA WHISK AND TEA BOWL

The tea whisk (*chasen*) is made of freshly split bamboo and should be warmed first, and at the same time checked to see if all the tines are intact. The tea bowl should also be warmed, since a cold bowl does not produce good tea. This is performed by pouring hot water into the tea bowl and immersing the whisk in it. The bowl is then wiped dry with a *chakin*, or white linen cloth.

MAKING THE TEA

Making good tea is the most important part of the tea ceremony, for no matter how skilled the *temae*, it will be in vain if the tea does not taste good. The quality of tea depends on the correct ratio of hot water to tea. In making *koicha* (thick tea), three heaped scoops of tea (1/8 ounce / 3.5 grams) are required per person, and in *usucha* (thin tea), only half that amount is needed. It is said that the best *koicha* results when the correct amount of tea for three to five persons is made in one bowl.

When boiling water is added to the tea in the bowl, the mixture is blended with the tea whisk, and here again the procedure is different for *koicha* and *usucha*. In the case of thick tea, the whisk is moved slowly and rhythmically, just enough to blend the tea into a smooth, thick liquid. In *usucha*, the tea is whisked briskly until it is frothy. This requires perhaps fifteen to twenty strokes. Too much whisking will make it too foamy and too little will leave it watery. One can only determine the best consistency with practice.

In making *koicha*, the amount of water added to the powdered tea makes a great deal of difference to both the taste and the consistency. If too little water is added, it will be impossible to achieve the right texture, and if more water is added later to make up for the lack, the taste will suffer. In the olden days it was said that a person needed the experience

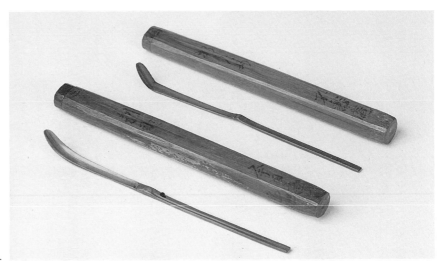

of making one *kanme*'s (8 1/4 pounds / 3.75 kilograms) worth of thick tea before they could make it properly. At the rate of one tea ceremony held for five persons once a week, this would mean that one would have to practice this art for five years before producing a good cup of tea.

The temperature of the hot water is another factor that will determine the tea's taste. This is dependent on the season, and small adjustments are made to accommodate changes in weather. In spring, for example, one ladle of cold water is added to the kettle just before the tea is made to reduce the water's temperature slightly. In winter, when the fire pit is used, boiling water is poured straight onto the tea.

It is also important to use the freshest possible tea. The color and flavor of tea change if it is not kept in a container that is properly sealed. On very humid days, moisture forming in the tea can change the flavor. For special occasions it is safest to use only the newest tea.

WASHING THE BOWLS AND THE WHISK
After the tea is drunk, the bowls are handed back to the host, who rinses them with a little hot water. When the main guest says to the host that the guests have had enough tea, the host rinses the tea bowl again and the tea whisk.

WIPING THE TEA SCOOP AND REPLACING THE UTENSILS
Next, the tea scoop is wiped with the *fukusa* and the host returns all the tea utensils he used for the ceremony to their original positions. He does this neither too hurriedly nor too slowly. He varies the speed of his movements throughout the ceremony. A good host is one who can hold the interest of his guests for the duration of the ceremony. When the ceremony is over, the guest should come away feeling satisfied with both the excellent tea and the beauty and tranquility of the performance.

NATSUME
Lacquered tea containers usually for thin tea.

CHA-IRE
Ceramic tea containers. They come with drawstring pouches made of precious fabric. Used for thick tea.

Admiring the Tea Utensils

When the tea has been drunk and all the utensils that have been used have been either rinsed or wiped, the host covers the water jar with a lid to signify the end of the ceremony. At this point the guests may ask the host for permission to examine the articles used.

If *usucha* was served, the chief guest will ask to see the lacquered tea container, called *natsume*, and the tea scoop, and if *koicha* was served, he will ask the host for the ceramic tea container, known as *cha-ire*, the tea scoop, and the pouch that held the *cha-ire*.

After examining each article, the main guest passes these on to the others for their observation. The host, in the meantime, waits outside with the door closed so that the guests can peruse the utensils in peace.

When the guests have looked at the different items, they return them to the host's place, and this is the signal for the host to reenter the room. He answers questions from the guests about the tea utensils. In formal tea ceremonies, this is an integral part of the performance, and the host will only use articles that are likely to provoke interested queries.

Etiquette for the Guest

Since the tea ceremony is such a formal affair bound by many conventions, there are also rules to be observed by the guest. These are briefly listed below.

Attire

A hundred years ago, kimono were the only clothing worn to a tea gathering, but nowadays, when most Japanese wear Western clothes in their daily lives, it is no longer obligatory to wear kimono. However, if one does wear kimono it is usual to wear a formal kimono with family crest. A man wears kimono with *hakama*, a divided skirt. He may also wear a *jittoku*, a short kimono coat, without *hakama*. A long kimono coat is not permissible in the tea room. With Japanese clothing, a clean pair of split-toed socks (*tabi*) should be worn. If not clad in kimono, a man would be wise to wear a suit and tie or something equally formal. A woman foregoing traditional dress should consider a dress or skirt that covers her knees when she is kneeling, and a clean pair of white socks over her stockings. Jewelry and other accessories are normally removed before entering the tea room to prevent then knocking the tea utensils. It is also better not to wear perfume that would jar with the smell of incense and spoil the ambience of the tea room.

Personal Items

It is appropriate for the guest to bring a folding fan (*sensu*), not for cooling himself, but to use for greeting the host and the other guests. A *tenugui* (rectangular cotton hand towel) or handkerchief should be brought by the guest to wipe his hands after washing at the water basin. The guest should also bring a pack of soft paper called *kaishi* to use when eating the sweets, and to wipe the rim of the tea bowl, and a *kobukusa*, a small square of brocade cloth on which to rest the tea bowl when drinking.

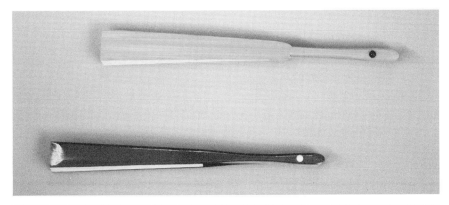

Folding fans.

KAISHI, FUKUSA

Kaishi paper, which all guests carry with them, and three types of silk cloth, including the *fukusa* (used by the host for wiping the utensils), the *kobukusa* (a small square of brocade cloth used by the guest to place the tea bowl on), and the *ōbukusa* (a larger version of the *kobukusa*, used for the same purpose).

Behavior

It is considered impolite to be late for a small *chanoyu* gathering that is set for an appointed time. When a large number of guests has been asked to a day-long ceremony it is not important to arrive on time, but in the former case it is good manners to arrive twenty minutes before the ceremony starts.

It is not proper to enter rooms other than the room where the tea ceremony is to be held. Usually places that are not open to the guests are indicated by placing a small bound stone on the stepping stone that leads in that direction or a bamboo pole across the entrance to the room or garden path. When walking through the garden people should always use the stepping stones so that they do not trample the moss or grass.

Smoking is generally prohibited at these gatherings. A smoking box, or *tabako bon*, is still provided, but this has become a decorative item. Sometimes there are designated places for the guests to smoke and they can do so by asking their host's permission.

It is customary to maintain absolute silence during the ceremony, while the guest observes the movements of the host making tea. If there are any questions, only the chief guest speaks, since all verbal exchanges are conducted in a prescribed form. After the *koicha* ceremony, when the atmosphere becomes more casual, the guests are at liberty to converse with one another or to smoke if they wish. But above all, proper dignity and manners should be observed, and at no time should anyone talk or laugh excessively in a way that might disturb the atmosphere.

When the tea utensils are presented for viewing, unless a guest is very experienced, he should avoid touching the articles for fear of damaging them or spilling the contents on the tatami floor. But it is up to the host to present his tea articles in such a way that the inexperienced guest will be given clues as to how to handle them properly.

Sweets

At all tea ceremonies, sweet cakes (*kashi*) are served before the tea. Moist cakes, usually made from sweet bean paste, are called *namagashi* and most often accompany thick tea, while *higashi*, small dry sweets with a sandy texture, appear with thin tea. At *koicha* gatherings, except for the very informal ones, it is usual for the special type of meal called *kaiseki* to be eaten before the sweets are served. After the guests have eaten the sweets, they go out of the tea room and rinse their mouths before coming back in again so that the mouth is refreshed in preparation for the tea.

The sweets are usually served on individual plates, the size of a saucer, and handled with a cake pick made of soft wood from the spice bush. The guest places the plate in front of his knees and transfers the cake to the soft paper (*kaishi*) he brings with him. The cake pick serves as a knife to cut the sweets into bite-size pieces before eating. Sometimes, when the

FUTAMONO
Lidded box for sweets.

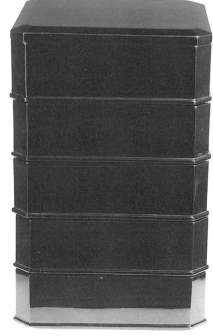

FUCHIDAKA
Tiered container for sweets.

HIGASHI-KI
Lacquered tray for the dry
sweets called *higashi*.

HACHI
Ceramic dish for moist sweets.

number of guests is uncertain, several pieces of cake are placed in a bowl (*hachi*) or lidded container (*futamono*), both made of porcelain. Special chopsticks are provided to pick up the cakes.

It is also customary before eating to ask the permission of the other guests to eat first by saying, "*O saki ni,*" or "Please excuse me for going before you." If the bowl containing the sweets is not placed directly in front of you, you should move it so that it is. Take out your *kaishi* and place a cake on it with the chopsticks. Should the tips of the chopsticks become sticky in the process, they should be wiped first with the paper and then passed on to the next guest, but not before first admiring the bowl for a moment.

Lidded containers are used either to keep out the dust or to keep freshly steamed sweets warm. Sometimes a tiered, lacquer container called a *fuchidaka* is used to serve cakes. In this case, the chief guest takes the *kashi* in the bottom layer, the second guest takes one from the next layer, and so on. Cake picks placed on the lid are provided to pick up the sweets. The empty boxes are passed back to the host.

Higashi are usually served on a lacquered tray and passed around. It is usual, when there are two types of *higashi* on the tray, to take both, although not more than three pieces should be taken. As in *koicha*, you should excuse yourself for eating before the next guest.

How to Drink Tea

USUCHA

In some cases, tea is brought by an assistant to the host and placed before the guest, but at a small tea gathering, the guest will usually go to the host to receive the tea. If the room is small, that is, less than four-and-a-half mats, the guest should not stand up but should advance on his knees toward the host. He should also remember the original place where the bowl was placed, and return it to that spot after drinking the tea. Here is the step-by-step procedure for drinking tea when the bowl has been brought and placed before you.

Place the tea bowl outside the border of the tatami mat you are sitting on. If there is a guest who has been served before you, it is polite to say, "*O-shōban itashimasu*," or "Please allow me to share tea with you." And to the guest who has not yet been served, you should excuse yourself for drinking first.

You then turn to the host and address him with the words, "*O-temae chōdai itashimasu*," or "I'll partake of your tea." When the tea has been prepared outside the room and brought in by someone else, then this address is unnecessary.

Pick up the bowl with your right hand and place it on the palm of your left hand. Steady the bowl with your right hand, with the thumb facing you, and make a small bow as a sign of reverence.

With the bowl still resting on the palm of your left hand, gently grip the rim of the bowl with your forefinger and thumb and turn the bowl about ninety degrees clockwise. Take a sip and then comment on how good it tastes, while dropping your right hand on the tatami before your knees.

Drink the remaining tea, and when you come to the last sip, make a sharp sound as you sip the last drops of tea.

After drinking, the rim of the bowl should be wiped lightly with the soft paper from left to right, as you steady the bowl with your forefinger and thumb.

Picking up the bowl and placing it on your left palm, turn it counter-clockwise so that it reverts to the position it was in before you drank from it.

Place the bowl outside of the tatami border in front of you and, with your hands on the mat, take a moment to admire the bowl. The bowl can be picked up with both hands to view it more closely, although in this case it is not good manners to raise the bowl too high.

If no one comes to take away your bowl, pick it up and return it to the host so that the front faces him.

KOICHA

Koicha can be drunk with three or more guests together or with a single guest. The tea can either be served by an attendant or the guest can go to fetch it himself, but in either case a *kobukusa*, or piece of brocade cloth to rest the bowl on, is provided with the bowl.

The main guest places the bowl on the inside of the tatami border, between himself and the second guest. The main guest then addresses the others who will share tea, saying "Let us partake of the tea together."

The main guest places the *kobukusa* on his left palm and the tea bowl on top of it. If the brocade that he is presented with is very valuable, the guest will put it temporarily to the right of his knees and take out his own, and use this to rest the bowl on instead. Steadying the bowl with the thumb in front and the other fingers around the bowl, he bows his head to the host to indicate that he is going to taste the tea.

He turns the bowl ninety degrees clockwise, so that the front of the bowl now faces the host, and with the edge of the *kobukusa* pinched between the forefinger and middle finger of his right hand, he takes a sip of tea.

At this time the host will ask him about the taste of the tea, and the guest replies politely, and then takes two and a half more sips.

After three and a half sips in all, the guest places the bowl, with the *kobukusa* underneath it, in front of his knees inside the border of the tatami mat. He takes out piece of soft paper to wipe the rim of the bowl. Then he folds it and returns it to his kimono pocket. The bowl is then rotated so that the front of the bowl will face the next guest squarely.

He then passes the bowl to the next guest with the *kobukusa* underneath it. If the next guest is a member of the opposite sex, he will instead place the bowl on the tatami inside the border between himself and the next guest. When the bowl is passed, the two guests will turn to face each other momentarily, and return to their original positions after it is over. In either case, after the bowl has been passed to the next guest, the first guest bows and the second guest nods as a sign of acknowledgment. These actions are called *ukerei* and *ukerei* respectively.

The next guest repeats the actions of the first guest, although he does not take time to say anything to the host, for the tea should be drunk while it is hot.

When the second guest has taken one sip, the chief guest asks the host for the name of the tea he is serving and the district where it was grown.

When the last guest has finished the tea, indicated by a loud sip, the main guest asks for the bowl to be brought to him so that he may admire it. The bowl is wiped and brought to the main guest, who passes it around for inspection.

Hanging Scrolls and Flowers

A scroll (*kakemono*) and flowers always accompany the tea ceremony. They are placed in the alcove, or where no alcove exists, they are hung on one section of the wall. Occasionally, a flower vase can also be hung from the wall.

The scroll is usually only shown in the earlier part of the tea ceremony, to be removed and replaced by flowers in the latter half. This arrangement makes it easier for the guests to appreciate the art and the flowers separately, and it also serves to change the atmosphere of the room. In an evening tea ceremony, flowers may be displayed during the earlier part of the gathering.

When the guest arrives at the tea room, he goes directly to the alcove to examine the scroll before exchanging greetings with the host, since the host has taken considerable trouble in choosing a scroll for this particular season or occasion. When this is done, the guest goes to his seat, from where he greets the host, venturing some opinion on the beauty of the scroll. He will also express his gratitude to his host for having taken such pains to entertain him.

The function of the *kakemono* is best expressed by a quote attributed

Flowers arranged in a ceramic
vase, placed in the center of
the alcove because the scroll
is wide and short.

to Rikyū: "The most important tea utensil is the *kakemono*, because
through it the heart of the host and the guest come together."

There are primarily two types of hanging scrolls: calligraphy, of which
there are several kinds, *bokuseki*, *kohitsu*, *shōsoku*, *gasan*; and paintings,
which can be classified into *kara-e*, *suiboku*, or *nanga*. The word *bokuseki*
itself means calligraphy, but in the tea ceremony it specifically refers to
works done by Zen priests of the Sung and Yuan dynasties of China,
although today the works of the high priests of Daitoku-ji in Kyoto are
also referred to as *bokuseki*. The contents of these scroll writings can be
poems expounding Buddhist canons, the teachings of famous masters,
or simply the names of famous disciples. The works are hung in the
alcove to be appreciated for their beauty and so that their messages can

be absorbed by the guest. They are the most valuable type of hanging scroll used today.

Between the tenth and thirteenth centuries, many excellent specimens of calligraphy were produced, and they were later cut out and mounted individually to hang in the alcove. These were known as *kohitsu*. As Japanese literature began to flourish during this period, even emperors, court nobles, and women of letters produced excellent calligraphy when writing poems or songs. The *kohitsu* type of scroll was first used by Jōō in 1555, and even today, whenever *kohitsu* are hung in tea rooms, the mood is instantly suggestive of the graceful elegance of the Heian period.

Letters written by tea masters were also mounted on scrolls and displayed. Sometimes a work would be inscribed with critical remarks, and these were known as *gasan*. The words may have been written by the artist himself, or they may have been words of appreciation from several different people, usually expressed in poetic form.

Paintings hung in the alcove would usually be of birds, flowers, or landscapes, and during the Muromachi period the most precious were those of the T'ang, Sung, and Yuan painters in China. Perhaps the most valuable of all were the "Eight Views of the Xiao Xiang Region," which depicted the lake Donging in central China. These paintings exerted a strong infuence on Japanese ink painting in the succeeding years. Zen priests studied this art during their training, and their own works executed in the style of "Eight Views" were found to be suited to the tranquil atmosphere of a tea house.

As a result of this preference for works of art, Japanese schools of painting multiplied during this period, and a specific Japanese style of art evolved with the appearance of many brilliant compositions. Today, paintings are often hung in the alcove of the waiting room, while in the tea room calligraphy in line with the theme of the ceremony is displayed.

Since the scroll is an object for admiration, it is always mounted

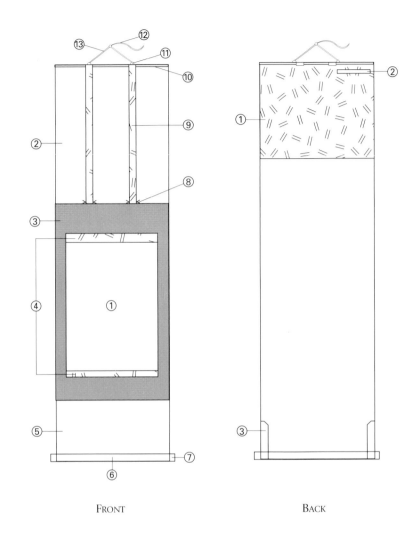

FRONT   BACK

MOUNTING FOR A TEA-ROOM SCROLL

A scroll is an artwork (frequently in the case of tea scrolls this is calligraphy alone), backed by paper and framed by two or three contrasting pieces of precious fabric, each of which is individually backed by paper. All pieces are laid flat and joined together with fine overlaps and then the whole length is backed with more paper. A thin rod is attached to the top end, and a rolling rod is attached to the bottom end. Tea scrolls usually have thin ornamental strips hanging from the top called *fūtai*, whose function is unknown, but which may have been to balance the overall effect of the scroll.

FRONT 1. Mounted work (*honshi*). 2. Upper mounting (*ten*). 3. Middle mounting (*chū-mawashi*). 4. Framing strips accenting bands above and below (*ichimonji*). 5. Lower mounting (*chi*). 6. Wooden rod as roller (*jikugi*) 7. Roller (*jiku*). 8. Little tassels on the end of the *fūtai* (*tsuyu*, literally "dew drop"). 9. Ornamental hanging strips (*fūtai*). 10. Top rod (*hyōgi*). 11. Metal rings for attaching the hanging cord (*kan/zagane*). 12. Binding cord (*maki-o*). 13. Hanging cord (*kake-o*).

BACK 1. Protective silk backing to protect the scroll when rolled up (*maki-ginu*). 2. Scroll title (*ge-dai*). 3. Strips of paper at either side of the lower end of the scroll to aid in rolling the scroll and help prevent the scroll from tearing (*jiku-dasuke*).

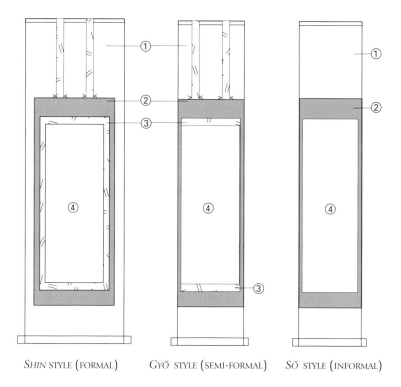

SHIN STYLE (FORMAL)   GYŌ STYLE (SEMI-FORMAL)   SŌ STYLE (INFORMAL)

DIFFERENT TYPES OF TEA SCROLL

All tea scrolls have the artwork framed by fabric or decorative paper, which in turn is framed by a contrasting fabric or paper. There are formal, semi-formal, and informal styles of scroll, and these are differentiated by whether or not they have decorative strips or frames around the artwork. Strictly speaking, the most formal style (*shin*) has the artwork framed all the way around with a precious fabric, the semi-formal type (*gyō*) has just two strips of precious fabric acting as accenting bands at the top and bottom of the artwork, and the least formal type (*sō*) has no accenting bands or frame at all. Famous artwork and Buddhist paintings have even more elaborate frames.

1. Basic mounting (*sō-beri*). 2. Inside mounting (*chū-beri*). 3. Decorative strips/frame (*ichimonji*). 4. Artwork.

thoughtfully. There are several styles of mounting, ranging from simple to intricate, depending on the type of materials used, and on whether it is a painting or a piece of calligraphy. Most of the scrolls used in tea rooms are mounted on paper, while the more elaborate ones are mounted on gold brocade or patterned silk. The mountings vary in keeping with the design of the tea room or the fame of the artist or calligrapher. Simple mountings are usually used for paintings and gold brocade for calligraphy, although some poems may call for more lavish, patterned silk instead. But by far the most important rule for the hanging scroll in the alcove is to see that it matches the proportions of the alcove itself, for no matter how well mounted the scroll may be, if it does not balance with the measurements of the alcove, the effect will be discordant.

Sen no Rikyū by Tanaka Senshō.

Making Thin Tea

This section focuses on the host's role in making thin tea (*usucha*) when a brazier is in use. The basic etiquette required of the guest is covered in the third sequence of this section, following the making of thick tea (*koicha*).

1. Holding the cold water jar, approach the sliding door to the tea room, kneel, set the jar down, open the door, and bow. Pick up the water jar in both hands, stand, and walk over to the brazier.

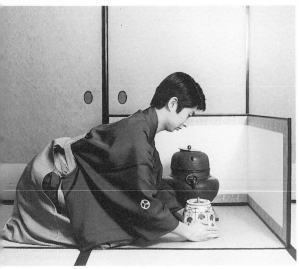

2. Kneel and then place the jar next to the brazier so that its center is in line with the lugs of the kettle.

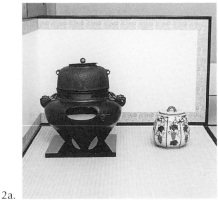

2a.

3. Hold the tea bowl (with the tea whisk and *chakin* inside and the tea scoop on top) in the left hand, and the tea container in the right hand. Place them in front of the water jar in one motion, leaving 1.5 to 2 centimeters (1/2 to 3/4 of an inch) between the tip of the tea scoop and the water jar.

3a.

4. Retrieve the waste-water receptacle (with the ladle rest inside and the ladle across the top) from the preparation area (*mizuya*). Carry it in your left hand. Take your seat ready to begin, setting the waste-water receptacle to your left (4a). Pick up the ladle in your left hand and hold it up, your right hand touching the end.

4a.

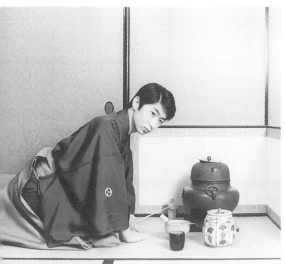

5. Take the ladle rest from the waste-water receptacle (not shown) with your right hand and place it at the left corner of the brazier. Set the ladle on the rest and bow to the guests, who will bow with you.

6. After moving the waste-water receptacle forward, compose yourself for picking up the tea bowl. Take the bowl with your right hand, transfer it to the left, then move your right hand forward so that you are holding the side of the bowl in the middle. Place the bowl in front of you, leaving enough space between your knees and the bowl for the tea container. In one motion, set the tea container down on the spot midway between your knees and the bowl.

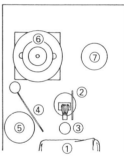

6a. Directly in front of the host (1) are the teabowl (2) and tea container (3), and to his immediate left the ladle (4) and waste-water receptacle (5). Set a little farther away, in a second row, are the kettle (6) and cold water jar (7).

7. Take the *fukusa* (square silk cloth) from your belt and fold it.

7a.

7b.

8. Pick up the tea container with your left hand. Wipe the top, then place the container in front of the water jar in the position where the tea bowl was previously.

8a.

9. Refold the *fukusa* in preparation for wiping the tea scoop. Pick up the tea scoop with the right hand and wipe it three times. The second time, wipe only the sides of the scoop. Lay the scoop on top of the tea container.

9a.

10. Still holding the *fukusa* in the left hand, take the tea whisk from the bowl and set it next to the tea container. Pick up the bowl with your right hand and move it slightly closer to you.

10a.

11. Grip the *fukusa* between your left index and middle fingers. Pick up the ladle with your right hand and lay it on your index finger, holding it in place with the thumb and index finger of your left hand. Slide the *fukusa* out with your right hand and use it to remove the lid of the kettle. (Men use the *fukusa* to lift the lid only on occasion.) Set the lid on the ladle stand, then set the *fukusa* aside. Still holding the ladle, take the *chakin* (cloth for wiping the tea bowl) from the bowl and place it on the kettle lid.

11a.

12. Lift the ladle by sliding your hand under the handle until you almost reach the joint, then bring your thumb around the top so that you are holding the ladle like a pencil. Take a half-scoop of hot water from the kettle and pour it into the bowl. Place the ladle on the far edge of the kettle's rim and lower the handle gently, changing the position of your fingers so that the thumb is now on the top of the handle just below the bamboo joint and the other fingers are underneath. This procedure for setting down the ladle is called *oki-bishaku*.

12a.

13. Pick up the tea whisk with the right hand and place it in the bowl so that your hand is resting lightly on the right-hand edge. Check the tines of the tea whisk as the water warms and softens them. Raise the whisk twice, rotating it towards you as you do so, all the time steadying the bowl with your left hand. Finally, whisk the water gently, drawing the *hiragana* character の in the bowl, then return the whisk to its upright position. This procedure is called *chasen tōji*. Pick up the bowl with the right hand, transfer it to the left hand, and pour the water into the waste-water receptacle.

13a.

14. Pick up the *chakin* with the right hand and wipe the rim of the bowl three and a half times and the base of the bowl twice as if you were drawing the *hiragana* characters い and り. Set the *chakin* in the bowl and put the bowl down in front of you, again with the right hand. Remove the *chakin* from the bowl and set it on the lid of the kettle.

15. Pick up the tea scoop with your right hand and the tea container with the left hand. Gripping the tea scoop between the ring and little fingers of the right hand, remove the lid of the tea container. Set the lid down in front of your right knee. Take two scoops of tea and place them in the bowl, holding the tea scoop as you would a pencil. Tap the scoop on the right edge of the tea bowl, replace the lid, then set the tea container back in front of the water jar. Replace the scoop on the lid of the tea container. Remove the lid of the water jar with your right hand and lean it against the side of the jar.

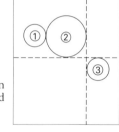

15a. The diagram shows the position of the bowl (2), tea container (1), and the tea container lid (3).

16. Pick up the ladle, holding it in your hand like a pencil. Draw a scoop of cold water and pour it into the kettle. Draw a full scoop of hot water from the kettle and pour about two-thirds of it into the bowl, returning what is left to the kettle. Set the ladle on the kettle, lowering it with your thumb extended underneath the handle and parallel with the ground and your four fingers raised neatly together. This procedure for setting down the ladle is called *kiri-bishaku*.

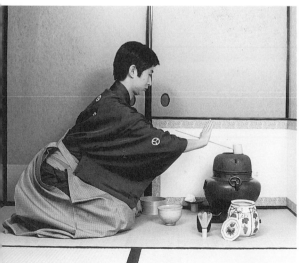

16a.

17. Steadying the bowl with your left hand, whisk the tea into a froth. When the tea is mixed, return the whisk to its place in front of the water jar.

17a.

18. Pick up the bowl with your right hand and place it on your left. Turn it clockwise so that the front of the bowl will be facing the guest when the tea is served.

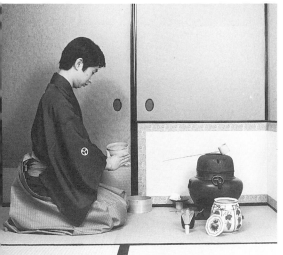

19. With your right hand put the bowl outside the edge of the host's mat.

19a.

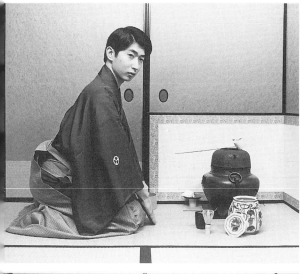

20. After the main guest has taken a sip, he or she will make a comment about the tea. Acknowledge this with a bow and tuck your *fukusa* back into your belt.

21. Add a scoop of cold water to the kettle. Replace the ladle on the kettle using the *hiki-bishaku* method: the tips of the fingers of the right hand slide almost to the end of the handle, then the thumb is brought around so that the palm is flat. When the fingers reach the very end of the handle, the thumb forms a circle with the fingers while the handle is gently laid down.

21a.

22. This ends the procedure for making tea. There are separate procedures for cleaning the utensils and returning them to their proper positions after the tea bowl is returned, and for presenting some of the utensils (usually the tea container and tea scoop) for closer inspection by the guests. When you end the ceremony, bow to the guests at the door before retiring.

Making Thick Tea

The following pages cover the procedure for thick tea (*koicha*) when
a fire pit is in use. Again, the focus is on the actions of the host.
For a description of the guest's role in the thick-tea ceremony,
consult the *Koicha* section of the *Temae* chapter.

1. Place the tea bowl (with the tea whisk and *chakin* inside and the tea scoop on top) in front of you and open the door to the tea room. With the bowl on the left palm, steadied by the right hand, stand and carry the bowl into the tea room. Take your seat and with your right hand place the bowl near the wall at left. Move the tea container slightly to the right in front of the water jar.

NOTE: The procedure illustrated here takes place in a tea room with Kyoto-size tatami mats, which are slightly larger than Kantō-size mats.

1a. The tea room alcove decorated with a hanging scroll and a vase of flowers for the ceremony.

1b. Before the guests enter, the cold water jar should be placed in the tea room with the tea container in front of it.

2. Pick up the tea bowl in your right hand, shift it to your left hand, and place the bowl next to the tea container in front of the water jar so that the three items form a triangle. Return to the preparation room (*mizuya*) and bring out the waste-water receptacle (with the ladle rest inside and the ladle on top), holding it in your left hand. After stepping into the tea room, turn around, kneel, place the waste-water receptacle in front of you, and close the door.

3. Holding the waste-water receptacle in the left hand, walk to the host's mat and take your seat, placing the waste-water receptacle at your side. Pick up the ladle in your left hand and hold it up in front of you with your right hand touching the end. Take the ladle rest from the waste-water receptacle with your right hand and place it just outside the host's mat near the lower right-hand corner of the fire pit (3). (The exact position is three rows of tatami stitching from each edge.)

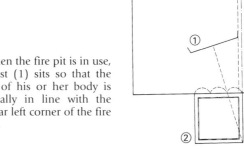

3a. When the fire pit is in use, the host (1) sits so that the center of his or her body is diagonally in line with the outer far left corner of the fire pit (2).

4. Put down the ladle, then bow to the guests, who will bow with you. Move the waste-water receptacle forward and compose yourself for picking up the bowl. Lift the bowl with your left hand, transfer it to the right and put it down in front of your knees, leaving enough room for the tea container. In one motion, place the tea container in the space between your knees and the bowl.

5. Untie the bow of the drawstring pouch. Turn the tea container counterclockwise ninety degrees, then spread out the drawstring gathers, first the far side, then the near side.

6. Pick up the container, and cupping the bottom in your left hand spread the sides of the pouch out further, first the right side, then the left. With your right hand, remove the container from the pouch and place it between the bowl and your knees. Take the pouch in both hands and straighten the material, then turn the pouch over, lay it in the palm of your left hand, and slide it onto your right hand. With your left hand, pick up the pouch from the bottom and place it near the waste-water receptacle.

7. Take the *fukusa* from your belt. Put your forefinger in the corner fold and allow the cloth to fall open. Holding the cloth over your left knee, examine each of its four sides in turn (this process is called *yo-hō-sabaki*), then fold it in preparation for wiping the tea container. Pick up the tea container with your left hand. Wipe the lid of the container in two parallel strokes (first the far side, then the near side), then touch the *fukusa* to the body of the vessel and rotate the container to clean. Set container between the water jar and the lower left-hand corner of the fire pit (7a). Fold the *fukusa* in preparation for wiping the tea scoop. Pick up the scoop with the right hand and wipe it three times. The second time, wipe only the sides of the tea scoop. Place the tea scoop on top of the tea container, on the side closest to the fire.

7a. The tea container (1), with the tea scoop laid across it, is positioned between the cold water jar (2) and the fire pit (3).

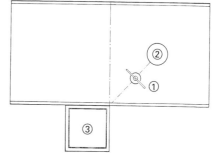

8. With the *fukusa* still in the left hand, take the tea whisk from the bowl with your right hand and place it next to the tea container. If the water jar has a lacquered lid, wipe the near side of it twice with the *fukusa*. Pick up the bowl with your right hand and move it slightly closer to you. Remove the *chakin* (cloth to wipe the tea bowl) from the bottom of the bowl and place it on the water jar lid. Grip the *fukusa* in your left hand between your left index and middle fingers. Pick up the ladle with your right hand and grip it with the thumb and index finger of your left. Slide the *fukusa* out with your right hand and use the cloth to remove the hot lid of the kettle and place it on the ladle stand. (Men use the *fukusa* to lift the lid only on occasion.)

9. Still holding the ladle, put the *fukusa* down near your right knee parallel with the edge of the tatami.

10. Shift the ladle to your right hand, gripping it like a pencil, and take a half-scoop of hot water from the kettle and pour it into the bowl.

11. Transferring the ladle to your left hand, replace the lid of the kettle with your right hand, using the *fukusa*. Replace the *fukusa* on the tatami and set the ladle on the stand. Pick up the tea whisk with the right hand and perform *chasen tōji* (*see* Making Thin Tea, step 13), then wipe the bowl with the *chakin* (step 14). Set the *chakin* in the base of the bowl and put the bowl down in front of you again with the right hand. Remove the *chakin* from the bowl and set it on the water jar.

12. Pick up the tea scoop with the right hand and the tea container with the left hand. Gripping the scoop with the ring finger and little finger of the right hand, remove the lid of the tea container with the same hand. Put the lid next to the tea bowl. Holding the scoop in the right hand as you would hold a pencil, take three scoops of tea from the tea container and place them in the bowl. Lay the scoop on the rim of the bowl and pour the rest of the tea (pre-measured to three scoops per guest) into the bowl, turning the container counterclockwise as you do so. Replace the lid of the container and return the container to its position with your left hand. Pick up the scoop and smooth out the tea in the bowl with the tip. Tap the scoop on the right edge of the tea bowl, then lay it across the lid of the tea container.

13. Pick up the ladle with the right hand and transfer it to the left. Use the *fukusa* to remove the lid of the kettle and place it on the ladle rest. This time put the *fukusa* next to your left knee.

14. Shift the ladle to your right hand, holding it like a pencil, and take a full scoop of hot water from the kettle. Pour enough into the bowl to blend the tea into a thick paste, then return the excess water to the kettle and lay the ladle, cup down, on the kettle. With the tea whisk, blend the tea slowly and rhythmically until it is smooth. Transfer the whisk to the left-hand side of the bowl. Pick up the ladle and take a full scoop of water. Holding the whisk over the bowl with the left hand, pour enough hot water over the whisk and into the bowl to make the correct volume of tea for the number of guests present (three sips per person). Lay the ladle back on the rim of the kettle. Blend the tea again until it is perfectly smooth. Return the whisk to its position.

15. Pick up the bowl with your right hand and place it on your left. Turn it clockwise so that the front of the bowl will be facing the guest when it is served. With your right hand, set the bowl outside the host's mat alongside the kettle lid. Take your *kobukusa* out and lay it next to the bowl.

15a. After the main guest has taken a sip, bow and ask how the tea is. Acknowledge the response with a bow. The main guest will pass the bowl to the next guest, who will drink, and pass the bowl down.

16. This ends the procedure for making thick tea. It is followed by the main guest asking the host the name of the tea and where it came from and who made the sweets. After the tea bowl is returned, the host cleans the utensils, returns them to their proper positions, and presents some of the utensils (usually the tea container, tea scoop, and drawstring pouch) for closer inspection by the guests. When you end the ceremony, bow to the guests at the door before retiring.

Etiquette for the Guest

Before entering a tea room, remove your watch, rings, and other jewelry, any of which may knock against or scratch tea utensils when you handle them. To take part in a tea ceremony, beginners bring a small folding fan (men's are slightly larger than women's), a packet of *kaishi* paper, and a cake pick.

Eating the Sweets

1. Before being served tea you will be offered sweets. When the sweets are passed to you, first bow slightly to the next guest and say, "*O-saki ni*" ("Please excuse me for going before you"). Pick up the sweets dish and draw it toward you while bowing slightly, then set the dish down. Take out your packet of *kaishi* and place it in front of you with the folded side closest to your knees.

2. If dry cakes are being served, use your fingers to pick up one of each variety and put them on your *kaishi*.

3. Pass the dish to the next person. Lift up the *kaishi* and eat your cake(s) with your fingers.

4. For moist cakes, use chopsticks to pick up the cake and put it on your *kaishi*.

5. Wipe the ends of the chopsticks on your *kaishi* and replace them neatly on the dish.

6. Pass the dish to the next person. Lift up the *kaishi* and eat your cake. If you are being served thick tea, wait until everybody has taken their cakes and the dish has been returned to the host's entrance by the last guest, then pick up your *kaishi* and use your cake pick to cut the cake into bite-size portions.

166

Drinking Thin Tea

1. If the host has an assistant, he or she will bring the tea bowl to you. Bow in response to his or her bow. Next bow to the guest to your right and say, "*O-shōban itashimasu*" ("Please allow me to share tea with you"), then bow to the guest to your left and say, "*O-saki ni*" ("Please excuse me for going before you").

2. Finally bow to the host and say, "*O-temae chōdai itashimasu*" ("I will partake of your tea").

3. Pick up the bowl with your right hand and place it on your left hand. Bow your head while raising the bowl slightly, in a gesture of thanks.

4. Turn the bowl clockwise on your palm so that the front now faces the host. To turn the bowl, grip the rim between your thumb and forefinger (4a).

5. After taking a sip, place the tips of the fingers of your right hand on the tatami and comment to the host on the taste of the tea.

6. Finish the tea with a sharp, audible sip. Wipe the rim with your fingertips from left to right (6a), then wipe your fingers on your *kaishi*.

7. Turn the tea bowl back counterclockwise so that the front of the bowl once more faces you, then place it beyond the edge of your tatami.

8. Now admire the bowl. With the tips of your fingers on the tatami observe the outside.

9. Pick up the bowl and look at the sides and foot, making sure to keep the bowl close to the tatami and being very careful not to let it slip. Place the bowl on the tatami again and observe it wistfully one more time before passing it to the next guest.

The Tea Ceremony as a Whole

A tea ceremony performance where up to five guests are invited at a time can roughly be divided into three stages.

In the preliminary part, called *zenseki*, the windows are shaded by bamboo screens to darken the room and a scroll alone is hung in the alcove. In special dawn or dusk tea gatherings, flowers may be placed in the alcove instead of a scroll. The guests enter the room and a simple *kaiseki* meal is served followed by sweets, after which the guests retire for a moment of relaxation in the inner garden. This recess and second stage is called *nakadachi*.

For the final stage of the tea ceremony, known as the *nochi-iri*, the scroll in the alcove is replaced by flowers, and the water jar, tea container, and some of the tea utensils are set out in the area where *temae* will be performed. The atmosphere of the room is quite different from the *zenseki* period as the bright, burning charcoal lights up the entire room and fills it with a pleasant aroma. The host picks up the ladle, a signal for his assistant to roll up the bamboo screen, brightening the room even further. The host performs *temae* in silence, while the guests concentrate on all his movements. This is the climax of the tea ceremony. The main guest will then speak, in special formal language, to his host, while the other guests remain silent. Once the *koicha* has been drunk, silence once more reigns. The sound of the boiling kettle subsides and the fire dies down. The host replenishes the charcoal, *usucha* is served, then the tea ceremony comes to an end.

On some occasions, after *koicha* has been drunk, the guests may be requested to move into another room where they are served with thin tea. Then the process of covering the flames does not take place. The whole event is characterized by great reverence, and appreciation of this encounter in one's life that will never be repeated, a sentiment that is expressed in the saying "*ichi go ichi e*," or "one chance in one's lifetime."

In keeping with the serious nature of the ceremony, it is customary for the host to change into clean clothes just before it, and for the guests

TABAKO-BON

The tobacco tray, containing a small ceramic brazier with a piece of hot charcoal embedded in ash, tobacco, pipes, and a bamboo tube into which ash is flicked from the pipe.

to arrive up to twenty minutes before the ceremony takes place. Most tea ceremonies are held at noon, but depending on the season and the occasion, they may also be held at dawn, early morning, between meals, in the late afternoon, in the evening, or at night. When an unexpected guest turns up, it can be performed at any hour.

It is the rule for the host to first invite his main guest, and then after consultation with him, select the other guests. The host also inquires whether the date and time he has chosen for *chanoyu* is convenient for the main guest before sending the invitations.

Preparations Made by the Host

THE TEA ROOM

Before a tea gathering, the host will make sure that the tea room is cleaned thoroughly and that the fire pit, the tatami mats, the linen tea cloth, the tea whisk, the ladle, and *fukusa* are all perfect and spotless. The chopsticks, the lid rest, the water pipe leading to the washbasin, and the chopsticks for the debris pit in the garden are all replaced by new ones made of fresh green bamboo. And finally he will make sure that all the tea utensils necessary for the ceremony are arranged in their proper places, so that the ceremony can start as soon as the guests arrive.

A small room near the gate in the garden is always provided for the guests to wait in before the start of the ceremony. A carpet is laid out there for them to sit on, and cups of hot water are provided for the thirsty. An iron kettle is placed on a brazier (*hibachi*). A tobacco tray is placed inside the waiting room with a container for loose tobacco, two Japanese pipes (*kiseru*), and a container with a small piece of burning coal embedded in ash to light the tobacco. There is also a device known as *haifuki* used for blowing away ash from the tobacco. One is not permitted to smoke inside the tea room unless invited to do so.

TE-ABURI

Small charcoal brazier used
as a hand warmer.

KAISEKI

The first course of the *kaiseki* meal consists of soup and rice served in
simple lidded bowls on a simple tray with a dish containing a delicacy
such as raw fish. This is followed by the *nimono*, which is considered the
main course. *Nimono* is a clear broth containing seasonal foods, often a
combination of dumplings, fish, poultry, vegetables, and tofu, the last
three of which appear in the *nimono* dish here.

THE INNER GARDEN

The inner garden, or *roji*, is swept clean in the morning and the grass and
shrubbery around the washbasin (*tsukubai*) cut and trimmed. The inside
of the basin is scrubbed and any stray stones around the basin are swept
away. Japanese straw hats and wooden sandals (*geta*) are made ready for
the guests in case of rain. The garden is sprinkled with water, the amount
usually varying according to the season. In winter, only the stepping
stones, or *tobi-ishi*, and the lower portion of the bamboo fence are sprinkled with water.

THE OUTSIDE WAITING AREA

The outside waiting area (*soto-machiai*) usually consists of a wooden
bench with straw cushions and a tobacco tray. In cold weather a hand-
warmer, called a *te-aburi*, or a *hibachi*, is used to keep the guests warm.

THE PREPARATION ROOM

This room (*mizuya*) is also thoroughly cleaned, and all the utensils
needed to make the charcoal fire and to serve the two kinds of tea are put
in their proper places before the beginning of *temae*.

THE MEAL

All items necessary for the *kaiseki* meal, which include lacquered trays or low tables, called *zen*, and the different types of bowls, plates, and other vessels, are prepared and kept ready. The tea ceremony can begin as soon as all the guests are assembled.

Various Types of Tea Ceremonies

THE NOON TEA CEREMONY (*Shōgo-no-Chaji*)

As this is the most formal of the different types of tea ceremonies, it serves as a good example to explain the different actions of the host and

MIZUYA

The *mizuya* (preparation room adjoining the tea room) contains shelves on which all of the utensils that are likely to be needed for the day's tea gathering are laid out in readiness. It has a bamboo-grated sink (40) a large water jar for washing (31), and pegs for ladles, whisks, and wiping cloths. There are separate wiping cloths for tea bowls, other utensils, and the hands.

1. Sharp-bladed knife for cutting flower stems (*kogatana*).
2. Small metal water pourer for adding water to the vase (*hana mizutsugi*).
3. Wooden tray for carrying flowers (*hana-dai*).
4. Large earthenware dish containing ash, for placing burning charcoal on, using metal chopsticks (*handa hōroku*); a long-handled scoop is used for scooping ash and smoothing the surface.
5. Metal fire pan with a wooden base for carrying burning charcoal, used behind the scenes (*dai-jūnō*).
6. Charcoal carry-box with wooden kettle stand, kettle rings, and single-feather duster, used behind the scenes (*hako sumitori*).

7. Tray for carrying incense appreciation utensils, consisting of a ceramic incense burner, miniature metal chopsticks and pincers, and a three-tiered lacquer box containing incense and a sliver of mica for heating it on (*kō-bon*).
8. Square black lacquered tray for carrying especially precious tea containers, etc (*yohō-bon*).
9. *Tenmoku* bowl on its own wooden stand (*tenmonku jawan to dai*).
10. Earthenware dish for carrying extra ash to add to the fire pit—damp ash in the cold months and ornamental white ash in the warm months (*hai hōroku* or *haiki*).
11. Charcoal basket, used for carrying charcoal into the tea room for the ceremony to add charcoal to the fire (*sumitori*).

12. Decorative incense container, used to carry incense into the tea room in the charcoal basket (*kōgō*).
13–15. Ceramic tea containers for thick tea (*cha-ire*).
16–18. Lacquered tea containers (*natsume*).
19. Tea scoops (*chashaku*).
20. Box containing utensils for sifting powdered tea and putting it into the tea container (*chahakibako*).
21. Extra cold water container lid (*mizusashi no futa*).
22. Cotton towel (*tenugui*).
23. Tea bowls (*chawan*).
24. Ladle/lid rests (*futaoki*).
25. Position for placing the lid of the cold water container (*mizusashi no futa*) while filling it.
26. Ladles (*hishaku*).
27. Linen cloths for purifying tea bowl in the ceremony (*chakin*).
28. Tea whisks (*chasen*).
29. Wooden square on which to stand the hot teakettle (*kamasue*).
30. Scrubbing brush (*shuronawa*).
31. Water storage jar (*mizutsubo*).
32. Water strainer (*mizukoshishaku*).
33. Water ladle (*mizu hishaku*).
34. Rag (*zōkin*).
35. Cloth for wiping tea bowl (*fukin*).
36. Waste-water receptacle (*kensui*).
37. Bowl for rinsing the linen cloths (*chakin-darai*).
38. Water replenishment pitcher (*mizu-tsugi*).
39. Cold water container (*mizusashi*).
40. Sink, covered with a bamboo grate (*nagashi*).

guests. During the stay in the *yoritsuki*, the guests appreciate the hanging scroll and change into clean white socks (*tabi*) in preparation for entering the tea room.

When all the guests have arrived, an attendant will guide them to the outside waiting area. The host, learning that everyone is present, goes out into the inner garden to rinse his mouth with water from the washbasin, carrying with him a wooden pail filled with water and a ladle. He scoops some water from the washbasin into the wooden pail and then pours all the contents of the pail into the basin, a signal to his guests that it is ready. He replaces the ladle and wooden pail in their original place in the garden and walks toward the middle gate to welcome his guests.

When the guests hear the host opening the middle gate of the outer garden, they advance toward him, and both host and guests greet each other with a silent bow. The host then shuts the gate and returns to the tea room, leaving the door of the small guests' entrance (*nijiriguchi*) partially open.

ROJI GETA
Wooden clogs for walking in the tea garden when it is raining or snowing.

ROJI ZŌRI
Straw sandals for walking in the tea garden in clement weather.

The guests follow the host to the middle gate and walk in single file toward the washbasin to wash their hands, at the same time observing and admiring the garden and scenery.

The main guest then walks along the stepping stones toward the tea room, crouches on the stepping stone in front of the tiny entryway, and slides back the open door to enter head-first. After entering the room he turns around and leans his straw sandals (*zōri*) against the lower wall outside the entrance, and the others do the same. The last person to enter slides the door shut with a small bang and locks it, a signal to the host that all are now assembled in the tea room. These preliminary rules are known as *seki-iri*, or rules for entering the tea room.

The host now comes out of his preparation room to welcome his guests verbally for the first time. His initial greeting is directed toward the main guest, who represents the whole party. When this is over the host returns to the preparation room, and brings out the utensils needed for changing the charcoal fire. He adds more coals to the fire in a procedure known as *sumi-demae*.

As the fire begins to burn, the guests are served with the meal known as *kaiseki*, which usually takes thirty to forty minutes, during which time the fire grows hot enough for the host to start the preparations for *koicha*. The host demonstrates his skills in the arrangement of charcoal in the fire so that it burns just strongly enough to boil the water in the kettle at exactly the right temperature at just the right time. (In the warmer months, when the fire pit is not used, the host waits until the meal is over before he heats the portable brazier.)

The *kaiseki* meal is only meant to quell the pangs of hunger and not to be a full meal, since the tea should be the highlight of the gathering. There is one ritual involved in the eating of the *kaiseki* called *sakazukigoto*,

Charcoal cut into prescribed lengths especially for use in the tea ceremony. The bigger piece of each pair is for use in the fire pit and the smaller for use in the portable brazier.

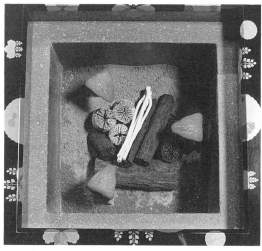

SUMI (RO)
Charcoal has just been added to the coals in the fire pit in the *sumi-demae* ceremony.

SUMI (FURO)
Charcoal has just been added to the coals in the portable brazier in the *sumi-demae* ceremony, and a crescent shape scooped from the front of the ash.

and that is the sharing of one saké cup between the host and his guests, which adds a fraternal feeling to the occasion. In a formal tea gathering, the cup takes a zigzag course between the host and all his guests, but on some occasions, the cup is only exchanged between the host and the main guest. This practice varies according to the type of guests present and the amount of time available.

When the meal is over, the guests replace all the bowls and dishes in their original positions on the tray and drop their chopsticks on the tray with a sharp clack. The host, who does not share the meal with his guests except to drink with them, will know that the meal is over and emerges from his seated position behind the host's entrance to the tea room to collect the trays. Everyone is silent during this interlude, and a sense of tranquility pervades the room. The main guest must now concentrate on the actions of the host, for it is one of the aims of *chanoyu* to bring the feelings of host and guests into perfect harmony.

If it is a tea ceremony during the warmer months, the host then adds charcoal to the portable brazier and cuts out a crescent-shaped piece of ash from the specially smoothed ash in the brazier, using a special spoon.

When the fire pit is used, the ash is rougher, and dampened ash is sprinkled around the edges to introduce cooler air and encourage the fire to grow.

The charcoal used to boil water is usually cut into small, uniform pieces, the size depending on whether the fire pit or the standing brazier is used. The size of the charcoal pieces determines the time it will take to create the correct temperature to boil the water.

THE DAWN CEREMONY (*Akatsuki-no-Chaji*)
This kind of ceremony is most often held in winter when the fire pit is in use. The first part of the ceremony is usually over before dawn, with the guests entering the tea room between three and four in the morning. (In earlier times this ceremony was known as *zantō-no-chaji* because the stone lanterns around the inner garden would still be alight.) The kettle is put over a charcoal fire started the previous evening.

Since the guests do not arrive at the same time, they are first offered thin tea as a prelude to the ceremony proper. Then fresh charcoal is added to the fire pit, and a *kaiseki* meal is served. Thick and thin teas follow as usual.

In this kind of ceremony the changing of the approaching dawn plays a very important role, and any delay can spoil the event. A host has to be very experienced in order to hold an early-morning ceremony, while the guest has to be equally experienced to fully appreciate it.

THE EVENING CEREMONY (*Yobanashi-no-Chaji*)

This type of ceremony is held on long wintry nights in order to enjoy leisurely conversation between the host and guests. Tea is first served, followed by the making of the charcoal fire, and the *kaiseki* meal is then eaten. After the thick tea and thin tea are drunk, there is another ceremony called *tomezumi*, in which the host continues to add charcoal to the fire as required while he talks with the guests and all enjoy the pleasant crackle of charcoal. It is normal, on these occasions, to light the room with lanterns made of wood and paper, and because of this, flowers are not used to decorate the alcove, since the light distorts their natural colors. However, if the season is right, white plum blossoms or white narcissus can be displayed.

THE EARLY MORNING CEREMONY (*Asa-cha*)

This is only held in the summer months, usually between five and six in the morning before the heat of the day sets in. The host moves quickly throughout the ceremony and it ends in about half the time of a usual ceremony.

"AFTER MEAL" TEA CEREMONY (*Hango-no-Chaji*)

This tea is held before or after lunch. Guests have eaten or will eat shortly, consequently only sweets are served. *Mochi*, cakes made of glutinous rice, or another more substantial confectionary is served since a *kaiseki* meal is bypassed. After the sweets, a bowl of clear soup will be drunk and a cup of saké passed around. Before *koicha* is served, the guests retire to the garden (or occasionally to another room) to wash their hands and relax. This is a contracted form of the formal tea ceremony, the biggest difference between the two being that only sweets are eaten before the drinking of tea. The ceremony also finishes more quietly than usual.

TEA CEREMONY ESPECIALLY FOR VIEWING VALUABLE TEA ARTICLES (*Atomi-no-Chaji*)
On occasion, art dealers who have a strong working relationship with
the host may ask to view the tea articles, and if they are granted permission they can inspect the utensils after the ceremony. The "*ato*" in the
Japanese name for this ceremony refers both to the viewing period after
tea has been consumed and to the lingering traces of the ceremony itself,
whether it be, say, a mark on the tatami or a pleasant goodwill.

IMPROMPTU CEREMONY (*Rinji-no-Chanoyu*)
Impromptu ceremonies are held spontaneously when a friend arrives
unexpectedly from a distant land. Since the gathering is held without
prior notice, it is not necessary for everything to be orderly. The floor is
quickly swept and a kettle is placed over the fire pit or brazier. The guest
is informally invited into the room and greetings are exchanged with the
host. A simple meal of rice balls or something similar is speedily prepared and served on ordinary plates, and the tea utensils are not elaborate or numerous. One or two valuable utensils, perhaps the tea caddy or
scroll, are chosen especially for the pleasure of the guest, but the viewing
is generally rather informal.

Apart from the types of tea ceremonies mentioned above, there are other
ceremonies that can be held especially for the cold season, the hot summer, New Year's Eve (*joya*), felicitations (*shūgi*), memorial services (*tsuizen*),
and partings(*sōbetsu*). However, in general the differences among them
all are very slight.

Flowers in the Tea Ceremony
The special floral arrangement used for tea ceremonies called *chabana*
differs distinctly from *ikebana*, the traditional Japanese art of flower
arrangement. *Chabana* has its roots in the earliest type of formal flower
arrangement known as *rikka*, which is still used in large tea ceremonies

RIKKA

A *rikka* flower arrangement, one of the earliest forms of flower arrangement in Japan, in which each element has cosmic significance.

today, but *rikka* is not typical of *chabana*. In the early days of the tea ceremony it was normal to arrange flowers in an artificial, stylized way. Later on, the process was simplified and the old rules were ignored in favor of a new, less formal style, where the flowers were admired for their own beauty rather than for the method of arrangement.

At one stage in the history of the tea ceremony, the host performed *chabana* in front of the guests, and did this by placing flowers in a vase in the most natural way. (*Ikebana* uses the term *ikeru*, meaning to arrange, while *chabana* uses *ireru*, meaning to put in.) This also meant that only seasonal flowers would be used.

It was Rikyū who once said, "Arrange the flowers as you would find them in the fields," and his maxim is still followed by tea masters today. The flower vase is called *hana-ire*, which means a container in which flowers are placed, rather than *hana-ike*, used in *ikebana*, which means a container where flowers are arranged.

Other differences between *chabana* and *ikebana* may help to explain the philosophy behind the use of flowers in the tea ceremony. For instance, *ikebana* relies on an artificial arrangement to express natural themes. *Chabana* flowers are, however, arranged without any artifice and put simply in a vase in their natural state. From its earliest times, *ikebana* was used to express heaven, earth, and the universe through its arrangement (although today there is more emphasis on themes from nature), but the emphasis in *chabana* is placed on flowers in their natural state.

In *ikebana* the petals are sometimes plucked off to expose only the

CHABANA
A *chabana* flower arrangement. Camellia with *sanshuyu* (a member of the dogwood family) in a simple bamboo vase.

stamen and the pistil, or leaves and branches may be colored artificially. All this is forbidden in *chabana*. Neither can wood, metal, or stone be used to decorate the creation. Highly scented flowers are also avoided in *chabana*. Some of the flowers shunned include the sweet-smelling daphne (*Skimmia japonica*), the cockscomb (*Celosia cristata*), dahurian patrinia (*Patrinia scabiosaefolia*), the pomegranate (*Punica garanatum*), the cow lily (*Nuphar japonicum*), and the pot marigold (*Calendula officinalis*).

In former times seasonal changes were emphasized in *ikebana*, but modern greenhouses and rapid airfreight have put an end to that principle. Nowadays, practically all kinds of flowers can be found at a florist, regardless of the season, and for this reason, the seasonal theme has lost its importance in the art.

On the other hand, the rules of *chabana* are more rigid, and ideally, only flowers appearing early in the season are used in the tea room. Flowers in the garden or those picked in mountains or fields are preferred, and those cultivated artificially are not preferred. Tea masters used to say that *chabana* should be arranged "with one's feet," which meant that you should venture out to look for flowers yourself, not buy them from a shop.

In *chabana*, the flowers are only used for the duration of the ceremony—that is, about an hour—and as soon as they have played their part in the ceremony, they are discarded, unlike *ikebana*, where the flowers may be kept for a week or so. Thus flowers that are too hardy or too gaudy are never displayed in the alcove.

Ikebana and *Chabana*

THE DIFFERENCE BETWEEN ARRANGING AND PLACING

It usually takes time to arrange flowers for *ikebana*, but an experienced person is supposed to be able to arrange *chabana* in a matter of moments, while the flowers are still fresh. Too long a time spent on *chabana* might cause them to wilt.

The tea master will cut off all the unnecessary leaves and branches from the flowers, perhaps adding a twig for special effect. He then picks up those he has selected and arranges them in his hand before placing them in the vase, making only a few minor adjustments in the way they fall. Only a seasoned tea master is able to accomplish what seems to be an extremely simple procedure both quickly and beautifully.

Whereas *ikebana* allows the use of wires or *kenzan* spikes to help create the arrangement, in *chabana* it is considered improper to use tools of any kind, and usually the master bends and shapes the stems with his hand.

Ikebana also permits the use of several different types of flowers in one vase, or a bunch of the same flowers may be arranged together, while in *chabana* only one flower is normally used, sometimes two, depending on the size of the flower and the container. If more than one flower is used, only one flower plays the dominant role while the other acts as a prop and is either half-open or still a bud.

This rule was also originated by Rikyū, who encouraged the use of as few flowers as possible: "Flowers arranged in a small room should be single in number, or at the most, two." This is still heeded by tea masters today. One must allow for the careful appreciation of only one type of flower at a time, and for this reason, all obscuring leaves and twigs must be removed.

In *chabana* the flower vase itself is an object of appreciation. For instance, when a bamboo container is used, great care is taken that the cut surfaces on the front are not hidden from view. If a woven basket is used, the handle is left unobscured, and for this reason large blooms are generally avoided because they may detract from the vessel's appearance. In *ikebana*, on the other hand, the vessel does not play such an important part, since the stress is more on the flowers themselves.

There are four different locations in the tea room where a flower vase may be placed. It may be placed on the tatami mat in the alcove, hung on the alcove wall or on the alcove pillar, or suspended from the alcove ceiling.

The first position, in which the flower vase is placed in the alcove either slightly to the left or to the right of the scroll, came about because of the old custom of placing an incense burner in the center of the alcove in front of the Buddha figure or Buddhist scroll. A candlestand was set to the right and the flowers to the left. Sometimes when the alcove was planned in reverse order, the flower container would naturally be placed on the right. Today, a thin board is usually placed under the vase, but if the alcove is not covered with tatami, no boards are necessary. If the scroll is very wide, the vase can be placed in the center of the alcove floor. In a very small tea room, the vase can be hung in the center of the alcove wall once the scroll is removed. In this case, a nail hidden behind the scroll and flush with the wall is pulled partially out and the vase is hung, usually about three feet (one hundred centimeters) above the floor of the alcove.

When both flowers and scroll are displayed at the same time, the vase can be hung from a nail in the pillar facing the guests' entrance.

Sometimes a special boat-shaped container (*tsurifune*) is used. Originally imported and made of metal, the form is now produced domestically and made from either bamboo or pottery. The whole arrangement is suspended from the center of the alcove ceiling.

Another important aspect is balancing the flowers with the vase. For example, the spread of the flowers should be larger in diameter than the

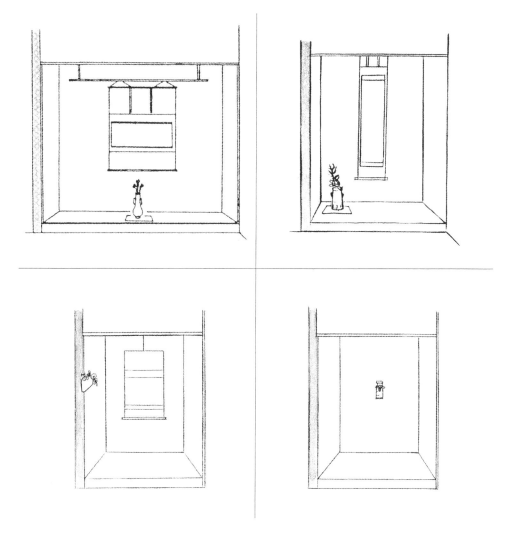

PLACEMENT OF THE FLOWER CONTAINER
The flower container is only set in the center of the alcove when the hanging scroll is wide and short. With a long hanging scroll, the vase should be placed to the left or right of the scroll. The vase rests on a thin lacquered or bare wooden board depending on how formal the arrangement is. A flower vase can also be hung on the back wall of the alcove.

mouth of the container and their length should be less than twice the height of the container. Finally, when the flowers have been placed in the vase, water is sprinkled on them to convey a feeling of freshness.

INCENSE
The first smell to greet you when you enter a tea room is the strong, sweet aroma of incense, which masks the smell of charcoal. The type known as *kōboku* (aromatic wood) is used with the brazier, and blended

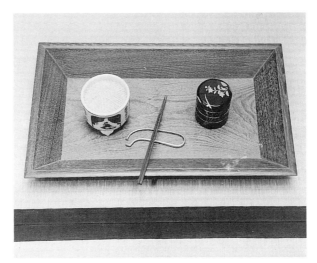

INCENSE APPRECIATION UTENSILS
A ceramic incense burner, miniature metal chopsticks and
pincers, and a three-tiered lacquer box containing incense
and a sliver of mica for heating it on.

incense, or *nerikō*, is used with the fire pit. There are two different ways of
burning incense: either by placing it directly in the fire (*shokō*), or placing
it near the fire and burning it slowly (*kunkō*). Sometimes the incense is
separated from the fire by a thin piece of mica. This procedure is known
as *monkō* and is only used on very special occasions. There are also two
types of incense burners, one called *soradaki-kōro*, used to perfume the
entire room, and a small one called *kikigōro*, which is picked up by the
guests.

CONCLUSION
The Tea Ceremony Today

By the late 1980s Japan had achieved, in the economic realm, its most cherished goal since Meiji times: to catch up with the advanced nations of the West. In embracing Western science, technology, and political systems, the Japanese achieved a level of modernization similar to that of many Western nations. Japan looked more Western, but beneath the surface major differences remained. In its acceptance of things Western, for example, Japan stopped short of adopting the sort of Western-style dichotomous thinking that pits nature against art, mind against body, or mankind against machines.

A comparison of gardens East and West illustrates the different approaches. In the clipped, geometrical gardens of Versailles, every detail is seen as an expression of human volition, while in a Japanese garden the intent is rather to incorporate nature as one element. The tea ceremony assumes the same approach, seeking to incorporate nature as represented in the seasons. The implements, decorations, and themes of tea change with the seasons. In fact, the form of the ceremony even changes depending on the time of day. Alterations in nature are considered of utmost importance.

Tea implements must, of course, work on several levels. Not only does a seasonal element play a role, but they must have a visual appeal while at the same time serving a functional purpose. A tea bowl, for example, conveys the tea from the host to the guest; it is lifted and brought to the lips, thereby stimulating the senses of taste, touch, and sight—in fact, all the senses—to broaden the tea experience.

Impressions received during the tea ceremony are to be accepted on their own merit. The human body, receptor of myriad sense impressions, is not seen as something that distorts the judgement of the intellect, but as a fundamental and trustworthy part of what it means to be human. Out of the separation of mind and body grew the notion that mental functions are superior to physical. But in a world where mind and body are multidimensional, the workings of the body—with all the senses functioning at heightened levels—can be taken as expressions of spirituality.

A certain humility accompanies this reaching out for the spiritual. When the host prepares for the tea ceremony by cleaning, readying the ash, and so on, he or she is engaging in what would in the West be classified as menial labor. Perhaps even the preparation of implements and the whisking of the tea itself might be regarded as better relegated to someone other than the host. It is characteristic of the tea ceremony, however, that the degree of cleaning undertaken, and the manner in which the host performs his labors, are themselves objects for admiration.

Many of the utensils used in tea are considered art objects worthy of the same respect and appreciation accorded in the West to, say, a painting. Tea bowls, tea containers, and flower vases all fall within this category, even given their functional purpose. In the West, an art collection mirrors the taste and personality of the collector's eye. The practitioner of tea, however, is no mere collector of art objects. Rather, he selects pieces not only in accordance with their inherent beauty but with an eye toward how they can be used in the tea ceremony. In choosing pieces for a given ceremony, a number of considerations—the season, the chosen theme, compatibility with other utensils, those in attendance— must all be accounted for before the host presents guests with a portion of his art collection (tea implements). The manner in which this is done is indicative of the host's feelings for the guests, who respond with a sincere effort to take in and appreciate the scope of the host's efforts. They do not focus narrowly on the collection itself, but seek rather to take in the totality of the way in which the host has arranged the experience on their behalf. As the tea ceremony proceeds, moreover, they must communicate their understanding and appreciation through their dealings with the host. The value of a guest's response is determined not by surface wittiness but by depth of sincerity. When pursued in earnest, the tea ceremony thus becomes an occasion for intense, full-scale personal involvement.

In the West, the question of the nature of human beings is often approached by stipulating what is *not* human: attention focuses on differences between humans and other creatures, or between humans and their creator. In the tea ceremony, people are seen primarily as beings who engage in acts of communication. First they must see to all aspects of their surroundings with scrupulous care, then physically prepare the tea and serve it to others. In so doing, they deepen their understanding of themselves. A study of the tea ceremony also reveals aspects of the Japan that existed prior to the urgent Westernization of the Meiji period. Even then, however, the West was not entirely unknown.

Contact between Japan and the West dates from the latter half of the sixteenth century. During subsequent centuries of self-imposed isolation, a trickle of contact with foreigners continued under strictly regulated conditions, until the country's gates were thrown open in the late nineteenth century. The tea ceremony is a product of Japanese culture that developed and flowered from the time contact with the West first began, throughout the years of virtual isolation. One might perhaps be forgiven for seeing in it various aspects of native culture which a Japan awakened to self-consciousness by exchanges with the West might have wished to preserve. But Japan in the sixteenth century knew nothing of Western technology. It was only when it saw the West in the process of industrializing during the late nineteenth century that Japan resolved to take the same road.

The economic success Japan achieved in the early 1990s can be seen as a fulfillment of the country's goals in the Meiji period. At the same time, however, Japan suffered loss in its headlong rush to catch up with the West. Recent experience has amply demonstrated that neither complacency nor mindless material consumption are answers to that loss.

The resulting sense of emptiness and purposelessness has brought about an unprecedented interest in things of spiritual or intangible value. As the pace of modern life quickens, some Japanese are stepping back to reevaluate their own cultural heritage, and this reassessment has led to a heightened interest in the tea ceremony.

As we move into the twenty-first century, it is important to remember that what is preserved of Japanese life and culture will not necessarily be for the benefit of Japanese people alone. My own suspicion is that while new generations of Japanese rediscover the tea ceremony, people of other nations will discover it for themselves, possibly make it a part of their lives. Perhaps some will even be led to discover unsuspected points of similarity with the traditions of medieval Europe.

It is barely a century now since human beings first put their faith in scientific progress and technology. If, having thereby achieved unprecedented levels of prosperity, we now fall back, we will prove unequal to the essential task of supporting the planet's increased population. Simply rejecting what science and technology can offer is no solution. At the same time, we would do well to keep in mind that the age of science is so far the briefest chapter in the long book of human history. To satisfy the universal hunger for deeper answers to life's questions, it is only natural that attention should be focused on various spiritual traditions in the human experience. It is my hope that the tea ceremony may once again be seen as a means to a rich inner life.

APPENDICES

A Tea Chronology

YEAR	EVENT	TEA DEVOTEES
607	Japanese mission sent to Sui emperor of China	
618	Beginning of the T'ang dynasty of China (618–907)	
630	First mission from Japan sent to China under the T'ang dynasty	
710	Beginning of the Nara period (710–94); capital transferred to Nara	
729	Emperor Shōmu holds *incha*, a religious ceremony during which tea is served to the monks participating in the religious service	
760	The first work on tea, *Cha Ching*, is written by Lu Wu	
794	Beginning of the Heian period (794–1192); capital transferred to Kyoto	
815	Emperor Saga visits Karasaki, Ōmi, and is served boiled tea by the priest Eichū	
907	Fall of the T'ang dynasty of China	
960	Beginning of the Sung dynasty of China (960–1278)	
1053	*Ch'a Lu* is written by the Chinese calligrapher Tsan Hsiang	
1107	Chinese Emperor Hui Tsung writes *A General View of Tea*, which contains the first mention of the tea whisk	Myōan Eisai (1141–1215) Myōe (1173–1232)
1191	Myōan Eisai returns from China and was said to have planted tea in Hizen district, northern Kyushu	
1192	Beginning of the Kamakura period (1192–1333); seat of government moved to Kamakura	
1206	Myōe was said to have been given tea seeds by Eisai and plants them in Toganoo, Kyoto	
1211	Eisai writes *Kissa Yōjōki*, or *Tea-Drinking Is Good for the Health*	
1214	Eisai presents his book to the shogun Sanetomo and recommends powdered tea to him	
1215	Eisai dies	

1274	The Mongols attack northern Kyushu	Musō Soseki (1275–1351)
1279	Fall of the Sung dynasty of China	
1281	Chinese troops attack Iki and Tsushima, islands of northern Kyushu	Sasaki Dōyo (1295–1373)
1324	Emperor Godaigo's retainer holds a tea gathering	
1332	*Tōcha* gatherings gain popularity	
1333	Fall of the Kamakura government; civil war begins between the Northern and Southern dynasties	
1336	Ashikaga Takauji, founder of the Ashikaga shogunate, forbids tea gatherings with the passing of a new law, *Kenmu Shikimoku*	
1339	Ashikaga Takauji founds Tenryū-ji; Musō Soseki nominated the first chief abbot	
1343	*Tōcha* gatherings regain popularity after the ban is lifted	
1368	Fall of the Yuan dynasty and start of the Ming dynasty (1368–1644) of China	
1392	Japan's Southern and Northern dynasties united after sixty years of war; Muromachi period (1392–1573) begins	
1397	Kitayamadai (now known as the Golden Pavilion of the Kinkaku-ji) is constructed by Ashikaga Yoshimitsu in Kitayama, Kyoto	
1416	Retainers of Prince Fushimi hold a tea gathering	Murata Shukō (1422–1502)
1467	Civil war (Ōnin no Ran) resumes and the Daitoku-ji is burned down	Furuichi Harima (1459–1508)
1469	A *rinkan* tea ceremony is held by Sumitane	
1476	*Kundaikan Sōchō-ki* is written by Nōami; contains drawings and descriptions of tea utensils and ink paintings	
1482	The Ginkaku of Jishō-ji (Silver Pavilion) is constructed by Ashikaga Yoshimasa at Higashiyama, Kyoto	
1490	Death of Ashikaga Yoshimasa	
1502	Death of Murata Shukō	Takeno Jōō (1502–55)
1533	Matsuya Hisamasa starts the *Record of Tea Gatherings*	Tsuda Sōtatsu (1504–66)
1540	Sen no Rikyū becomes a pupil of Takeno Jōō	Tsuda Sōgyū (?–1591)
1548	Tsuda Sōtatsu starts *Diary of Tea Gatherings*	Imai Sōkyū (1520–93)
1549	Francis Xavier comes to Japan	Sen no Rikyū (1522–91)
1554	Imai Sōkyū records his own tea ceremonies	Oda Nobunaga (1534–82)
1555	Takeno Jōō dies	Toyotomi Hideyoshi (1536–98)
1565	Tsuda Sōgyū records all the tea gatherings to which he was invited, an account he continues until 1587	Shimai Sōshitsu (1539–1615)
		Sen no Dōan (1546–1607)
		Sen no Shōan (1546–1614)
1573	Defeat of the Ashikagas by Oda Nobunaga brings about the end of the Muromachi period and the beginning of the Azuchi-Momoyama period (1573–1603)	Tokugawa Ieyasu (1542–1616)
		Yamanoue Sōji (1544–90)
		Furuta Oribe (1544–1615)
		Oda Uraku (1547–1621)

1582	Nobunaga is forced to commit suicide by Akechi Mitsuhide, who is in turn defeated in battle by Toyotomi Hideyoshi	Matsuya Hisamasa ((?–1598)
		Matsuya Hisayoshi (?–1633)
		Kamiya Sōtan (1551–1635)
1585	Hideyoshi is promoted to chief advisor to the emperor and holds a tea ceremony at a small palace inside the Imperial Palace. Rikyū receives the title *Koji*	Hon'ami Kōetsu (1558–1637)
		Hosokawa Sansai (1563–1645)
		Konoe Nobutada (1565–1614)
		Sen no Sōtan (1578–1658)
1586	Hideyoshi performs a tea ceremony at the Imperial Palace using his portable gold tea pavilion	Kobori Enshū (1579–1647)
		Kanamori Sōwa (1584–1656)
1587	Hideyoshi's palatial home, the Jurakudai, is built in Kyoto. The Great Tea Ceremony of Kitano is held, where Rikyū, Sōgyū, and Sōkyū act as *sadō*	Shōkadō Shōjō (1584–1639)
1588	Yamanoue Sōji begins to write the *Record of Yamanoue Sōji* (completed in 1590)	
1590	Death of Yamanoue Sōji	
1591	Rikyū is forced to commit suicide	
1592	Invasion of Korea	
1593	Death of Imai Sōkyū	
1597	Second invasion of Korea	
1598	Hideyoshi holds a cherry-blossom–viewing ceremony in Kyoto. Death of Hideyoshi	
1600	Battle of Sekigahara	
1603	Edo period (1603–1868) begins	Katagiri Sekishū (1605–73)
1607	Dōan dies	
1610	Furuta Oribe goes to Edo to serve the second Tokugawa shogun	
1612	Kobori Enshū constructs the Kohō-an in the Daitoku-ji	Fujimura Yōken (1613–99)
1614	Battle between the Tokugawas and the Toyotomis. Sen no Shōan and Konoe Nobutada die	
1615	Another battle between the Tokugawas and the Toyotomis in which the latter are defeated. Furuta Oribe is forced to commit suicide	
1616	Death of the shogun Tokugawa Ieyasu	
1618	Jo-an is constructed in the Kennin-ji by Oda Uraku	
1625	The Katsura Imperial Villa is completed	Yamada Sōhen (1627–1708)
1637	Death of Hon'ami Kōetsu	Sugiki Fusai (1628–1706)
1644	Fall of the Ming dynasty of China	Kusumi Soan (1636–1728)
1645	Hosokawa Sansai dies	
1647	Enshū dies	
1658	Sōtan dies	
1659	The construction of the Shūgaku-in Imperial Villa begins	
1665	Katagiri Sekishū becomes teacher of tea to the Tokugawas	
		Yabunouchi Chikushin
1680	Yamada Sōhen writes *Sadō Benmō Shō*	(1678–1745)
1700	Kusumi Soan writes *Chawa Shigetsu Shū*	

1706	Death of Sugiki Fusai	
1708	Death of Yamada Sōhen	Kawakami Fuhaku (1716–1807)
1787	Matsudaira Fumai writes *Kokon Meibutsu Ruijū,* in which he records all the famed tea utensils in existence	Hayami Sōdatsu (1727–1809) Matsudaira Fumai (1751–1818)
1793	The Kohō-an burns down	
1811	Matsudaira Fumai writes about the origins of Seto ware in *Seto-tōki Ranshō*	Ii Naosuke (1815–60)
1860	Ii Naosuke is killed outside the gate of Edo Castle	Okakura Kakuzō (1862–1913)
1868	Beginning of the Meiji period (1868–1912)	
1898	Dai Nihon Chadō Gakkai is founded by Tanaka Senshō	
1905	Tanaka Senshō publishes *Chazen Ichimi*	
1906	*The Book of Tea* is published by Okakura Kakuzō in New York	
1913	Okakura Kakuzō dies	

Tea Terms by Category
Japanese to English

---

1. Utensils / Decoration

懐紙	*kaishi*	paper for holding sweets and wiping the bowl
掛物	*kakemono*	hanging scroll
釜	*kama*	kettle
黒文字	*kuromoji*	cake pick
建水	*kensui*	wastewater receptacle
香木	*kōboku*	aromatic wood added to charcoal fire as incense
古帛紗	*kobukusa*	square cloth of precious fabric for resting tea bowl or precious items on
仕覆	*shifuku*	drawstring pouch mainly for thick-tea container
水墨画	*suibokuga*	ink painting
炭	*sumi*	charcoal
扇子	*sensu*	fan
台子	*daisu*	large utensil stand
棚	*tana*	small utensil stand
茶入	*cha-ire*	thick-tea container
茶巾	*chakin*	linen napkin for cleaning bowl
茶杓	*chashaku*	tea scoop
茶筅	*chasen*	bamboo tea whisk
茶箱	*chabako*	box containing a picnic set of tea utensils
茶碗	*chawan*	tea bowl
手拭	*tenugui*	rectangular cotton hand towel
天目台	*tenmoku-dai*	stand for *tenmoku* bowl
天目	*tenmoku*	tea bowl with a narrow foot and a broadish rim, originating in China
銅鑼	*dora*	metal gong
棗	*natsume*	wooden tea container, often lacquered, usually for thin tea
練香	*nerikō*	blended incense
灰	*hai*	ash in the fire pit or brazier
鉢	*hachi*	bowl for food or sweets
花入	*hana-ire*	flower vase
柄杓	*hishaku*	ladle
火箸	*hibashi*	long metal chopsticks for handling charcoal
火鉢	*hibachi*	brazier
帛紗	*fukusa*	square silk cloth for purifying utensils
蓋置	*futa-oki*	rest for lid or ladle

墨蹟	*bokuseki*	scrolls of calligraphy by Zen priests
水指	*mizusashi*	cold-water container
銘	*mei*	poetic name
楽焼	*raku-yaki*	raku ware

2. Ceremony / Process

薄茶	*usucha*	thin tea
主菓子	*omogashi*	main sweet
詰め	*tsume*	last guest
懐石	*kaiseki*	tea ceremony meal
客	*kyaku*	guest
濃茶	*koicha*	thick tea
後炭	*gozumi*	second of two procedures to add charcoal to the fire
正客	*shōkyaku*	principle guest
初炭	*shozumi*	first of two procedures to add charcoal to the fire
炭手前	*sumi-demae*	procedure for adding charcoal to the fire
膳	*zen*	meal tray
茶会 (ちゃえ)	*cha-e*	early name for tea ceremony
茶会 (ちゃかい)	*chakai*	tea gathering
茶事	*chaji*	full-length tea gathering including meal
茶花	*chabana*	a type of flower display for the alcove of a tea house
亭主	*teishu*	host
点前	*temae*	general term for the ritual preparation of tea or the procedures used in making tea
中立	*nakadachi*	short recess between *kaiseki* meal and *koicha* service
生菓子	*namagashi*	moist cakes
半東	*hantō*	host's assistant
干菓子	*higashi*	small dry sweets
風炉	*furo*	portable brazier
炉	*ro*	fire pit, sunken hearth

3. Tea House

茶道口	*sadōguchi*	host's entrance to tea room
書院	*shoin*	formal room for receiving guests, also a tea room style
障子	*shōji*	sliding screens covered in translucent paper
草庵	*sōan*	rustic hut-style tea house
台目畳	*daime datami*	special short tatami mat
畳	*tatami*	rush mat
違い棚	*chigaidana*	staggered shelves beside alcove for displaying writing utensils, incense burner, etc.
茶室	*chashitsu*	tea room
床 / 床の間	*toko / tokonoma*	alcove
躙口	*nijiriguchi*	narrow entrance to tea room, mainly used by guests

広間	*hiroma*	large tea room
襖	*fusuma*	sliding doors
水屋	*mizuya*	preparation room adjoining tea room
寄付	*yoritsuki*	room where guests first gather to prepare for tea ceremony

4. Garden

石灯籠	*ishi-dōrō*	stone lantern
腰掛待合	*koshikake-machiai*	waiting arbor
ごろた石	*gorota-ishi*	pebbles piled near stone washbasin
関守石	*sekimori-ishi*	stone bound with rope used to bar paths that guests should not follow
中門	*chūmon*	gate where host first greets the guests
塵穴	*chiri-ana*	pit for placing fallen leaves and other debris from the garden
つくばい	*tsukubai*	stone washbasin
飛び石	*tobi-ishi*	stepping stones
延段	*nobedan*	paved walkway
踏石	*fumi-ishi*	high stone at guest's entrance to tea room
前石	*mae-ishi*	flat stone in front of stone washbasin for standing on
待合	*machiai*	waiting room or waiting arbor
露地	*roji*	tea garden

5. Types of Tea Ceremonies

暁の茶事	*akatsuki no chaji*	dawn tea ceremony (winter)
朝茶	*asa-cha*	early-morning summer tea ceremony
口切りの茶事	*kuchikiri-no-chaji*	tea ceremony celebrating the breaking of the seal on a jar of new tea (November)
正午の茶事	*shōgo-no-chaji*	midday tea ceremony
初風炉	*shoburo*	first use of the portable brazier in the year (May)
名残りの茶事	*nagori-no-chaji*	tea ceremony honoring the last remains of the year's supply of tea and to see out the warm months before winter sets in (October)
初釜	*hatsugama*	first tea ceremony of the year
夕ざりの茶事	*yūzari-no-chaji*	early evening tea ceremony held in the warm months
夜咄	*yobanashi*	winter-evening tea ceremony

Tea Terms by Category
English to Japanese

1. Utensils / Decoration

ash in the fire pit or brazier	*hai*	灰
bowl for food or sweets	*hachi*	鉢
box containing a picnic set of tea utensils	*chabako*	茶箱
brazier	*hibachi*	火鉢
cake pick	*kuromoji*	黒文字
charcoal	*sumi*	炭
cloth of precious fabric for resting tea bowl or precious items on	*kobukusa*	古帛紗
cloth (silk) for purifying utensils	*fukusa*	帛紗
cold-water container	*mizusashi*	水指
fan	*sensu*	扇子
flower vase	*hana-ire*	花入
hand towel, cotton	*tenugui*	手拭
hanging scroll	*kakemono*	掛物
incense, blended	*nerikō*	練香
incense in the form of aromatic wood	*kōboku*	香木
ink painting	*suibokuga*	水墨画
kettle	*kama*	釜
ladle	*hishaku*	柄杓
metal chopsticks for handling charcoal	*hibashi*	火箸
metal gong	*dora*	銅鑼
napkin, made of linen, for cleaning bowl	*chakin*	茶巾
paper for holding sweets and wiping the bowl	*kaishi*	懐紙
poetic name	*mei*	銘
pouch with a drawstring; mainly used for thick-tea container	*shifuku*	仕覆
raku ware	*raku-yaki*	楽焼
rest for lid or ladle	*futa-oki*	蓋置
scrolls of calligraphy by Zen priests	*bokuseki*	墨蹟
stand for *tenmoku* bowl	*tenmoku-dai*	天目台
tea bowl	*chawan*	茶碗
tea bowl with a narrow foot and a broadish rim, originating in China	*tenmoku*	天目
tea container, often lacquered wood, usually for thin tea	*natsume*	棗
tea scoop	*chashaku*	茶杓
tea whisk, bamboo	*chasen*	茶筅
thick-tea container	*cha-ire*	茶入

utensil stand, large	*daisu*	台子
utensil stand, small	*tana*	棚
wastewater receptacle	*kensui*	建水

2. Ceremony / Process

fire pit, sunken hearth	*ro*	炉
first of two procedures to add charcoal to the fire	*shozumi*	初炭
flower display for the alcove of a tea house	*chabana*	茶花
full-length tea gathering including meal	*chaji*	茶事
general term for the ritual preparation of tea or the procedures used in making tea	*temae*	点前
guest	*kyaku*	客
host	*teishu*	亭主
host's assistant	*hantō*	半東
last guest	*tsume*	詰め
main guest, principle guest	*shōkyaku*	正客
main sweet	*omogashi*	主菓子
meal tray	*zen*	膳
moist cakes	*namagashi*	生菓子
portable brazier	*furo*	風炉
procedure for adding charcoal to the fire	*sumi-demae*	炭手前
recess between *kaiseki* meal and *koicha* service	*nakadachi*	中立
second of two procedures to add charcoal to the fire	*gozumi*	後炭
small dry sweets	*higashi*	干菓子
tea ceremony, early name for	*cha-e*	茶会 (ちゃえ)
tea ceremony meal	*kaiseki*	懐石
tea gathering	*chakai*	茶会 (ちゃかい)
thick tea	*koicha*	濃茶
thin tea	*usucha*	薄茶

3. Tea House

alcove	*toko / tokonoma*	床/床の間
entrance (narrow) to tea room; used mainly by guests	*nijiriguchi*	躙口
formal room for receiving guests, also a tea-room style	*shoin*	書院
host's entrance to tea room	*sadōguchi*	茶道口
preparation room adjoining tea room	*mizuya*	水屋
room where guests first gather to prepare for tea ceremony	*yoritsuki*	寄付
rush mat	*tatami*	畳
rush mat, special short size	*daime datami*	台目畳
shelves (staggered) beside alcove for displaying writing utensils, incense burner, etc.	*chigaidana*	違い棚
sliding doors	*fusuma*	襖
sliding screens covered in translucent paper	*shōji*	障子
tea house, rustic hut-style	*sōan*	草庵

| tea room | *chashitsu* | 茶室 |
| tea room, large | *hiroma* | 広間 |

4. Garden

gate where host first greets the guests	*chūmon*	中門
paved walkway	*nobedan*	延段
pebbles piled near stone washbasin	*gorota-ishi*	ごろた石
pit for placing fallen leaves and other debris from the garden	*chiri-ana*	塵穴
stepping stones	*tobi-ishi*	飛び石
stone at guest's entrance to tea room	*fumi-ishi*	踏石
stone bound with rope used to bar paths that guests should not follow	*sekimori-ishi*	関守石
stone in front of stone washbasin	*mae-ishi*	前石
stone lantern	*ishi-dōrō*	石灯籠
stone washbasin	*tsukubai*	つくばい
tea garden	*roji*	露地
waiting arbor	*koshikake-machiai*	腰掛待合
waiting room or waiting arbor	*machiai*	待合

5. Types of Tea Ceremonies

dawn tea ceremony (winter)	*akatsuki no chaji*	暁の茶事
early-evening tea ceremony held in the warm months	*yūzari-no-chaji*	夕ざりの茶事
early-morning summer tea ceremony	*asa-cha*	朝茶
first tea ceremony of the year	*hatsugama*	初釜
first use of the portable brazier in the year (May)	*shoburo*	初風炉
midday tea ceremony	*shōgo-no-chaji*	正午の茶事
tea ceremony celebrating the breaking of the seal on a jar of new tea (November)	*kuchikiri-no-chaji*	口切りの茶事
tea ceremony honoring the last remains of the year's supply of tea and to see out the warm months before winter sets in (October)	*nagori-no-chaji*	名残りの茶事
winter-evening tea ceremony	*yobanashi*	夜咄

Tea Utensils—Diagrams and Variations

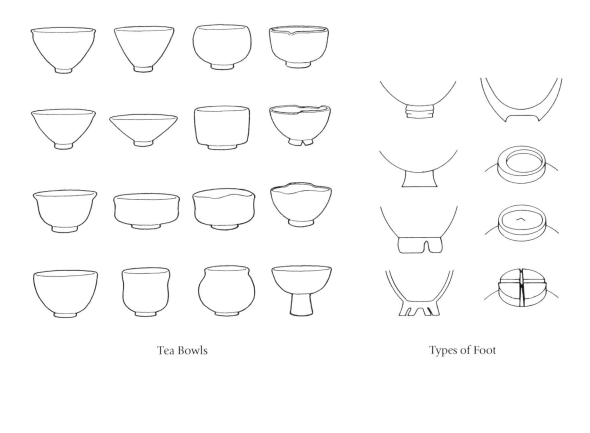

Tea Bowls

Types of Foot

Thin-tea Container (*usucha-ki*) Shapes

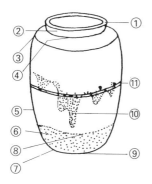

1. Lip (*kuchitsukuri*).
2. Neck (*koshiki*).
3. Shoulder (*kata*).
4. Join of neck (*koshiki-giwa*).
5. Lower body (*koshi*).
6. Exposed clay (*tsuchi*).
7. Skirt (*suso*).
8. End of the glaze (*yūdomari*).
9. Base (*soko*).
10. Glaze drip (*nadare*).
11. String mark around the center (*dō-himo*).

COMPONENTS OF THE *CHA-IRE*

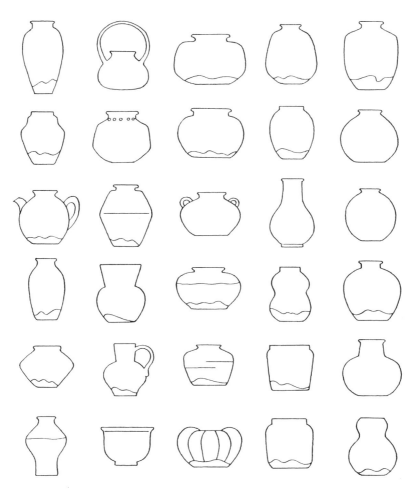

Thick-tea Container (*cha-ire*) Shapes

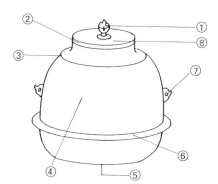

1. Knob (*tsumami*)
2. Mouth (*kuchi*)
3. Shoulder (*kata*)
4. Body (*dō*)
5. Base (*soko*)
6. Wing/skirt (*hane*)
7. Lugs (*kantsuki*)
8. Lid (*futa*)

COMPONENTS OF THE KETTLE (*KAMA*)

Kettle Shapes

Bamboo Flower Con-
tainers and Baskets

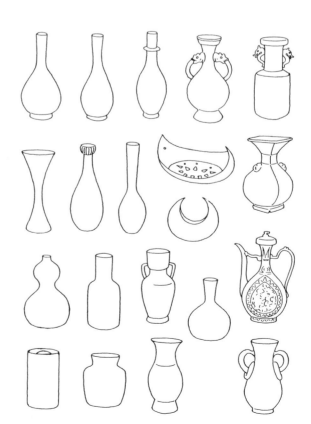

Metal and Ceramic
Flower Containers

Selected Tea Houses

Tea houses are listed by location, with the specific name following the name of the temple, shrine, or other compound in which they are located.

Daitoku-ji is a collective name designating the main temple and numerous small temples found within its compound, some of which possess tea houses mentioned below.

DAITOKU-JI: GYOKURIN-IN
KASUMIDO-NO-SEKI

This is found in the same building as the Sa-an (see below) but is designed in the larger *shoin* style. Its four-and-a-half-mat size makes it the smallest of the *shoin* tea rooms. The alcove is about two meters high, incorporating shelves and, below them, a scroll painting of Mt. Fuji. These shelves have been specially placed in order to give an impression that the summit of Mt. Fuji is shrouded in mist, for the name of the tea house literally means "room of mist." The architectural style is, more accurately, a combination of *shoin* and *sōan* features.

DAITOKU-JI: GYOKURIN-IN
SA-AN

The Sa-an tea house was constructed in 1741–42 by Kōnoike Ryōei. The design of the house was in keeping with the taste of the wealthy merchant class of the time, but it is interesting to note that an attempt has been made to preserve a *wabi* feeling by mixing cut rice stalks with mud to plaster the walls of the tea room. The pillar in the room is made of a red pine log whose bark has not been removed, and a thin wooden plank is placed between the tatami where *temae* is performed and the tatami where the guests are seated.

DAITOKU-JI: JUKŌ-IN
KAN'IN-NO-SEKI

A simple tea room built in the style that Rikyū cherished is located in the Jukō-in, a temple constructed in 1566 by Miyoshi Yoshitsugu and founded by the priest Shōrei. It is said that Rikyū used to sit and meditate in this temple, and his grave and those of his family lie within the temple grounds.

DAITOKU-JI: KOHŌ-AN
BŌSEN-SEKI

Originally built by Kobori Enshū, the Bōsen-seki was destroyed by fire in the mid–Edo period and reconstructed by Matsudaira Fumai. It is an excellent example of Enshū's originality and creativity, for the whole building is built to resemble a boat. The latticework sliding door above the porch looks like a boat's window, and is used not only to cut off the outside view but to prevent sunlight from entering the room from the west. Alongside the alcove there is a preparation area built according to the aristocratic taste of the time. The name comes from a poem by Chuang Tzu, the famous Chinese writer and philosopher.

DAITOKU-JI: KOHŌ-AN
SAN'UN-JŌ

This, like the Bōsen-seki, was also reconstructed at a later date, and is a good example of the style of tea room preferred by the nobility for their samurai guests. It is constructed in a mixture of *shoin* and *sōan* styles, and there are two entrances to the room, one through the inner garden, the other through the adjacent *shoin* room.

DAITOKU-JI: KŌTŌ-IN
SHŌKŌ-KEN

This tea room, simple in style and austere in decoration, was built by Hosokawa Sansai, a disciple of Rikyū who adhered to his master's teachings on *wabi*. He also ordered the construction of Kōtō-in, which was completed after his death. The present building today has been largely remodeled and bears little resemblance to the original.

DAITOKU-JI: RYŪKŌ-IN
MITTAN-NO-SEKI

The name of this tea house in the Ryūkō-in refers to a set of ink scrolls by Mi An Hsien Chieh (1107–86), a Chinese priest of the Rinzai school who is known in Japan as Mittan Kanketsu. A special alcove was reportedly designed exclusively to hang his ink scrolls, though whether it is actually an alcove is a matter of some dispute. The sole surviving scroll, harking back to the origins of the Rinzai school of Buddhism, is highly prized. A letter to Yamanoue Sōji attached to the scroll indicates a mount was once designed by Rikyū. The present mounting is by Kohori Enshū.

DAITOKU-JI: SHINJU-AN
TEIGYOKU-KEN

The tea room is built next to a reception room and is believed to be the work of Kanamori Sōwa. On entering the guests' entrance, there is an earthen floor where the sword rest and the washbasin are located, a peculiar feature of this house, since these two are usually found outside the tea room. The interior divides into two sections by means of a papered sliding door, which makes the room look larger than it is.

IMPERIAL PALACE (SENTŌ GOSHO)
YŪSHIN-TEI

The Yūshin-tei building in the garden of the palace originally belonged to the Konoe family, but was moved to its present location in 1884. The roof is made of thatch, and the large crescent window in the tea room makes it unusually light inside.

JISHŌ-JI (GINKAKU-JI): TŌGU-DŌ
DŌJIN-SAI
The Ginkaku-ji, or Silver Pavilion, was built by Ashikaga Yoshimasa, who had originally planned to decorate it with silver, but whose death put an untimely end to this project. Of the original edifices only the Ginkaku-ji and the Tōgu-dō, constructed in the fifteenth century and containing a special room for the temple's main Buddha image, have survived. The room in the Tōgu-dō called the Dōjin-sai is fitted with shelves, a side window, and a fire pit. It is four and a half mats in size. Believed to be unchanged since it was first built, the room was not originally intended to be used for tea.

KATSURA IMPERIAL VILLA
GEPPARŌ
This tea house was used more often for moon-viewing than for tea-drinking, and so the decor was kept very simple. The preparation room consists only of a fire pit and some simple shelves.

KATSURA IMPERIAL VILLA
SHŌKIN-TEI
The thatch-roofed Shōkin-tei is surrounded by deep eaves on three sides, and along the façade of the building is a porch where a cooking area, preparation area, and shelves are located. Usually the kitchen facilities are hidden from view, but in the Shōkin-tei they are boldly presented for all to see.

KŌMYŌ-JI: SAIŌ-IN
YODOMI-NO-SEKI
This tea house was built by Fujimura Yōken in the latter half of the seventeenth century and named after the Yodo River, which can be seen from the window. The host's area is separated from the guests by a dividing wall and a papered sliding door, a device named *dōan kakoi* after its inventor, Dōan, son of Rikyū. The sliding door is opened when all the utensils necessary for *temae* have been carried into the tea room, and closed when *temae* is over.

MANJU-IN
HASSŌ-KEN
This temple was originally constructed at the end of the eighth century and was transferred to its present location in the mid–seventeenth century, since which time a small and large *shoin* room, a tea house, and a garden have been added. The style of the tea room is very similar to that of the Hassō-no-kakoi of the Katsura Imperial Villa, since its owner, Prince Ryōshō, was related to the Hachijō princes, builders of the Katsura Imperial Villa in Kyoto.

MYŌKI-AN
TAI-AN

This tea house is frequently attributed to Rikyū, but this has never been verified. Yet the bold composition of the tea room and its *wabi* atmosphere strongly suggest the hand of the great master. The walls in the alcove are covered with mud, a style created by Rikyū. Of all *sōan*-style tea houses in existence, the Tai-an is the oldest, and it has been designated a National Treasure.

NANZEN-JI: KONCHI-IN
HASSŌ-NO-SEKI

The tea room was designed by Enshū in 1628 at the request of the abbot of Konchi-in, and is separated from the drawing room by a pair of papered sliding doors. Although the word *hassō* implies that there are eight windows, the tea room has only six. Unlike most tea houses, the passage leading to the guests' entrance does not go through the inner garden, but along the porch.

NINNA-JI
HITŌ-TEI

This tea room was built at the end of the eighteenth century at the command of Emperor Kōkaku. Although the design of the room conforms to *sōan* patterns and has a thatched roof, the tea room has two separate entrances, one of which was used exclusively for the nobility. The ceiling is rather high and has a round window, another reflection of contemporary aristocratic taste.

NINNA-JI
RYŌKAKU-TEI

This building was originally in the garden of a private residence and was transferred to the temple during the first half of the nineteenth century. The tea room is identical in design to the Jo-an tea room in Inuyama City, Aichi Prefecture. Next to the tea room there is another room, which is not screened off by sliding doors, and both can be used in combination to form a large tea room.

NISHI HONGAN-JI
IKUJAKU-NO-SEKI

This tea room is believed to have been originally attached to the Hiunkaku, which was built by Hideyoshi in his Jurakudai palace. Ikujaku-no-seki was removed to its present site later on. The first-recorded tea ceremony took place in 1795. The structure has large windows beside the alcove overlooking the pond in the garden. Near the guests' entrance, there is an area of wood flooring where the lords' retainers would sit. Shelves used for making tea are also built next to the guests' entrance.

ROKUON-JI (KINKAKU-JI)
SEKKA-TEI

The temple formerly belonged to the Saionji family, but in the fourteenth century it was purchased by Ashikaga Yoshimitsu, who made it into a mountain retreat. The tea house was designed by Kanamori Sōwa in a country style with thatched roof, earthen floor, and a built-in fireplace. At the end of the nineteenth century the Sekka-tei was destroyed by fire, but it was reconstructed soon afterward according to the original design.

SAIHŌ-JI
SHŌNAN-TEI
This is a building in the garden of the temple, with a tea room located in one corner. The building itself is said to have been restored around the beginning of the seventeenth century by Sen no Shōan, who planned to retire there in his old age. Although it is built in the *sōan* style, there are papered windows and doors that can be opened to view the scenery in the garden, unlike other *sōan* tea huts. The temple is popularly known as Kokedera, or Moss Temple, because of the thick layer of moss that carpets the entire garden. It is planted with beautiful trees and carefully laid out with a pond to enhance the view.

YABUNOUCHI HOUSE
EN'AN
This tea room is located within the residential quarters of the principal of the Yabunouchi School of Tea in Kyoto. It was originally built by Furuta Oribe, but was destroyed by fire in 1864 and rebuilt three years later. It is designed in the *sōan* style with a thatched roof, and one of its unusual characteristics is a triple *roji*, meaning there are three parts to the tea garden.

TOKYO
SENSŌ-JI: DENPŌ-IN
TENYŪ-AN
The tea house was built by a tea devotee from Nagoya and was transferred twice before it found its final home in the Sensō-ji, in Asakusa, Tokyo. It was styled after the Fushin-an, a tea house owned by the Omotesenke School of Kyoto, and is one of the oldest replica of the Fushin-an in existence today.

OSAKA
MINASE SHRINE
TŌSHIN-TEI
The Minase Shrine is located near the palace of the former emperor Gotoba, who, after abdicating, often went to the palace to view the moon and the beautiful scenery around the palace. In the Edo period, the former emperor Go-mizunoo built a tea house in that area. It is constructed in the *sōan* style, but its interior is more lavish, with an alcove, shelves, and large windows. The ceiling is exposed and woven in a lattice pattern from seven different types of grass.

KANAZAWA, ISHIKAWA PREFECTURE

YŪGAO-TEI

The present tea house was remodeled from an earlier construction, in the grounds of what is now Kenroku-en garden. The tea house is built beside the pond and contains a very bright, three *daime datami* tea room.

MATSUE, SHIMANE PREFECTURE

KANDEN SAN-SŌ

KANDEN-AN

This tea room was built in 1792 by Matsudaira Fumai, in the grounds of the villa of his chief retainer, in order to enjoy tea after his duties as feudal lord were done for the day. Fumai would enter the tea room after he had had a bath and changed from his hunting clothes. Unlike the Enshū style, Fumai's tea rooms are famed for their simplicity. The Kanden-an is one of very few tea rooms in existence today that was designed by Fumai.

KANDEN SAN-SŌ

KŌGETSU-TEI

The Kōgetsu-tei is located next to the Kanden-an and was built around the same time. The fire pit is built into the *daime* tatami, and the shelves next to the alcove are of a highly original design. The style reflects a combination of *wabi* and the samurai taste of the time. The garden is covered with pebbles and laid out with stepping stones, and the view of the moon from the garden is especially beautiful.

INUYAMA, AICHI PREFECTURE

JO-AN

This tea house was built by Oda Uraku in 1618 inside the grounds of the Kennin-ji in Kyoto. It was transferred to Tokyo in 1908, and then to Ōiso, Kanagawa Prefecture, and finally to Inuyama in 1972. It has one unusual aspect, which is a bamboo pole across its window, and the lower portion of the walls are covered with old paper calendars.

Glossary

akatsuki-no-chaji: the name of the dawn tea ceremony held during the coldest season of the year. Guests arrive between three and four in the morning, before sunrise. Dawn breaks during the ceremony.

asa-cha: the early-morning tea ceremony held before the sun gets too hot for comfort during the summer months.

bokuseki: scrolls of calligraphy written by Zen priests, usually conveying philosophic ideas. Some of the oldest examples, most cherished by tea masters, date back to the Sung dynasty of China in the eleventh century.

chabako: literally "tea box." Contains all the tea utensils, except the waste-water receptacle, brazier, and kettle, necessary for the ceremony.

chabana: flowers arranged in the alcove of the tea room. Differs from *ikebana* in its use of only one or two flowers placed by the host in a simple container to appear just as they would in the field.

cha-e: an early name for the tea ceremony, which originated from the practice of tea-drinking in Buddhist temples and gradually spread to the general populace toward the end of the fourteenth century. As the etiquette of tea-drinking developed, various names were given to the ceremony, one of which is the more popular *chanoyu*.

cha-ire: the container for powdered tea, used only in the making of *koicha*. There are various styles and shapes, but they are almost always ceramic, and contained in a drawstring pouch (*shifuku*) of precious fabric. *See also "natsume."*

chaji: a full scale tea ceremony that includes a ritual or rituals for adding charcoal to the fire, a *kaiseki* meal, and preparation of both *koicha* and *usucha*.

chakin: the piece of white linen used for wiping the tea bowl before and after tea is served. It is soaked beforehand, wrung, and folded in a prescribed manner.

chasen: the bamboo whisk used for blending or whisking the powdered tea after water has been added. It is warmed in water first to prevent the fine bamboo tines from splintering during use.

chashaku: the long, curved scoop used for taking powdered tea from the caddy to the bowl. Originally these scoops were made of either ivory or metal, but now they are most often made of bamboo. Most tea masters carve their own, and many come in a container that bears the name of the carver, the poetic name given to the scoop, and some facts relating to its history. It is customary to use the most appropriately named tea scoop for a special tea ceremony.

chashitsu: literally "tea room." Shape, size, design, and decoration vary according to current fashion. Today there are two kinds, the large room (*hiroma*) and the small room, the latter of which is used most frequently.

chawan: the tea bowl. Unlike its Western counterparts, the tea cup and coffee cup, the Japanese tea bowl has no handle. Bowls for tea are made in a size and shape suitable for holding in both hands.

chigaidana: staggered shelves built beside the alcove in a *shoin*-style room, where writing utensils, an incense burner or incense container, or even books are displayed.

chiri-ana: a small pit dug into the ground close to the tea house into which fallen leaves from the inner garden are placed with long bamboo chopsticks. Its purpose is both practical and ornamental, and to enhance its attractiveness, a stone is embedded in the edge and a pair of long green bamboo chopsticks laid against it.

chūmon: the middle gate built between the inner and outer garden where the host greets his guests before the start of the tea ceremony.

daime datami: a tatami mat, shorter than the usual tatami.

daisu: utensil stand now used for grand, formal tea ceremonies. Originally introduced from China, it is made from either plain or lacquered wood, and differently named according to its shape or design.

dora: a metal gong that is struck as a signal for the guests to either enter the tea room, or, after a short recess, reenter the room.

fukusa: a square silk cloth used to clean the tea container, tea scoop, and other utensils before tea is made and before they are inspected by guests. The host can also use it to pick up the hot lid of the kettle. *See also "kobukusa."*

fumi-ishi: high stone at the guests' entrance to the tea house. Usually great care is taken to choose a large stone with a flat top. The small flat stones lined up in front of the bench in the waiting arbor are also called by this name.

furo: the portable brazier used during the warmer months to heat the kettle. Can be made from iron, bronze, silver, or ceramics, and is named according to its shape and size.

fusuma: sliding wooden doors in a traditional Japanese house, covered with plain or decorated paper.

futa-oki: ladle or kettle lid rest, made of bamboo, pottery, metal or glass. Bamboo *futa-oki* are often made by the host for the day's tea gathering.

gorota-ishi: a mass of variously shaped pebbles piled up between the stone washbasin and the stone on which the guest stands to wash his hands.

gozumi: a procedure for adding charcoal to the fire for the second time in a full-length formal tea gathering. The first is called *shozumi*.

hachi: a bowl or other type of container in which food or sweets are served.

hai: ash, usually referring to the ash bed in the portable brazier or fire pit in which the fire is laid. The ash is sculpted into elegant forms, which are also admired as part of the overall art of the tea master.

hana-ire: a flower vase most commonly made of pottery, metal, or bamboo. Either placed on the alcove floor, hung on the pillar beside the alcove, on the wall, or suspended from the alcove ceiling, depending on the size of the tea room.

hantō: the host's assistant.

hatsugama: the first tea ceremony of the year; usually held on the fifth or sixth day after New Year's Day.

hibachi: a brazier in the waiting room on which a kettle is placed.

hibashi: a pair of long metal chopsticks used for rearranging the coals in the fire and placing fresh pieces of charcoal on the fire.

higashi: small, dry cakes with a sandy texture served mainly with *usucha*.

hiroma: name applied to a room larger than eight mats suited to larger gatherings of guests. The design of the room differs from that of the smaller tea room, and there may be shelves next to the alcove for displaying precious objects.

hishaku: bamboo ladle for drawing water in the tea ceremony.

ishi-dōrō: a stone lantern originating in China initially used in the gardens of temples and shrines. In the early Muromachi period it was placed in ordinary gardens for decoration, or to illuminate the garden during evening tea ceremonies.

kaiseki: literally "warm stone," this is the light meal served at the start of the tea ceremony before *koicha* is drunk, so named because monks in Buddhist training placed small heated stones on their stomachs to quell the pangs of hunger when fasting. The meal usually consists of rice, two kinds of soup, and three fish or vegetable dishes, and is accompanied by saké.

kaishi: soft sheets of paper used either for holding sweets or for wiping the rim of the tea bowl before passing it on to the next guest. The *kaishi* used by men is slightly larger than that for women.

kakemono: hanging scroll mounted with a work of art or calligraphy that decorates the tea room alcove.

kama: the kettle used for boiling water, usually made of iron, although silver and gold kettles are also produced. They are often called by the name of the area in which they are made or after the owner or craftsman.

kensui: wastewater receptacle, used during the tea ceremony to discard the water used to rinse the bowl.

kōboku: pieces of aromatic wood, including aloeswood and sandalwood, added to the charcoal fire in the portable brazier in the warmer months. Pieces of aromatic wood were first imported from China, and incense appreciation was later adopted as one of the formal procedures of the tea ceremony.

kobukusa: square of elegant cloth on which the tea bowl is rested when drinking tea. It is used only when *koicha* is drunk and is usually made of a precious fabric such as heavily patterned brocade. *See also "fukusa."*

koicha: literally "thick tea." Powdered green tea made with a higher ratio of tea to water than for *usucha* (thin tea), for a thicker consistency. The tea used for *koicha* is of the highest quality, made from the new leaves of tea shrubs that are protected from direct sunlight during the final days before harvest.

koshikake-machiai: waiting arbor, usually a small arbor in the garden where guests wait for the host to greet them before the ceremony begins. It is considered proper to provide a waiting room in the outer garden as well as a waiting arbor in the inner garden, but in less formal tea ceremonies, a single waiting room or arbor can serve both functions.

kuchikiri: a special tea ceremony celebrating the breaking of the seal on the jar that contains the year's new supply of tea. This tea is procured in leaf form from the tea dealer and stored in a large sealed ceramic jar called a *chatsubo*. It is customary to perform the ceremony of breaking the seal and grinding the leaves into powder in the month of November.

kuromoji: cake pick traditionally used for eating cakes in the tea ceremony; whittled from the wood of the spice bush.

kyaku: guest. In a tea gathering the principle guest (*shōkyaku*) and the last guest (*otsume*) have the hardest roles to perform. The principle guest represents all the other guests in asking the host questions about the day's gathering and the utensils used. The last guest must support the principle guest by clearing up all used dishes and helping to return utensils to the host.

machiai: waiting arbor, or waiting room. *See also "koshikake-machiai."*

mae-ishi: the stone placed just in front of the stone washbasin where the guests crouch to rinse their mouths and wash their hands with water.

mei: poetic name given to especially highly valued utensils. Utensils with names that suit the occasion or season of a tea ceremony are favored. The guests are expected to ask the host about the provenance of each tea utensil, including its poetic name.

mizusashi: a lidded water jar, most often used for replenishing the kettle with cold water; made of pottery, metal, glass, or wood.

mizuya: a small room or nook containing shelves and a washing area where all the utensils needed for a tea gathering are laid out ready for use.

nagori: literally "a lingering parting." By October, the year's supply of tea is almost at an end, and warm days are about to give way to cold, so tea performed in this month pays special attention to the quiet melancholy of parting.

nakadachi: the short recess between the *kaiseki* meal and the *koicha* service, during which time the guests relax for a while in the waiting arbor in the inner garden or the waiting room while the host sweeps the tea room and makes other preparations for the second part of the tea ceremony.

namagashi: soft cakes, usually made of sweet bean paste, eaten mainly before *koicha*. *See also "omogashi."*

natsume: the lacquered tea container used to hold *usucha*. Originally, only certain shapes of tea containers were so named, but gradually all lacquered tea caddies came to be referred to as *natsume*. *See also "cha-ire."*

nerikō: blended incense that is placed in the charcoal fire in the colder months when fresh coals are added to the fire.

nijiriguchi: literally "crawling entrance." The narrow entrance to a tea house through which one has to crawl to enter.

nobedan: a paved walk in the garden surrounding the tea house; made of natural or hewn stone carefully arranged in geometric patterns.

omogashi: the main sweet, i.e., the sweet usually eaten before drinking *koicha*. *See also "namagashi."*

raku ware: this most renowned of all tea-ceremony ceramics is produced in a district near Kyoto. It is soft and fashioned by hand without a potter's wheel. Until recently, the bulk of raku ware was the work of generations of artists in the Raku family, which was favored by Rikyū. Chōjirō, Kōetsu, and other famous artists have left a number of masterpieces of raku pottery.

renji mado: a window with two papered sliding screens and a bamboo latticework frame outside it.

ro: a fire pit, sunk into the floor of the tea room and used during the cold season in place of the portable brazier. It imparts a feeling of warmth and coziness to the room in the cold months.

roji: literally "dewy path." This is the inner garden of the tea house where there are stepping stones, a waiting arbor, and a stone washbasin. More elaborate tea gardens have both an inner and an outer *roji*.

sadōguchi: the host's entrance in the tea room.

sekimori-ishi: small stones bound with hemp rope that are placed on stepping stones in the *roji* where there are forks in the path, to show guests which path to follow and which path not to follow.

sensu: a folding fan, placed in front of the knees when making formal greetings in the tea room. A fan placed before a person's knees signifies his respect for those present.

shifuku: drawstring pouches used to couch ceramic tea containers or tea bowls, usually made from silk brocade, satin damask, or silk crepe. *Shifuku* are themselves objects of appreciation.

shoburo: the first time that the portable brazier is used in the year, in May.

shōgo-no-chaji: midday tea gathering. Midday is the most common of all times to invite guests for tea.

shoin: originally this was a study or writing room in a Zen temple occupying a small, projecting section of the building, but later it was adopted into the design of private homes where the *shoin* room replaced the drawing room, and ornamental shelves and alcoves were added. Later on, a desk was also incorporated into the design, usually located just beneath the window.

shōji: translucent paper-covered sliding screens, used as windows or doors in traditional Japanese homes.

shōkyaku: the principle guest. *See "kyaku."*

shozumi: a procedure for adding charcoal to the fire in the early part of the tea ceremony performed in front of the guests. *See also "gozumi."*

sōan: a tea hut built from only natural materials to resemble a rustic farmhouse; used for the simplest, least affected style of tea ceremonies.

suibokuga: ink paintings. They were popular in the T'ang and Sung dynasties of China and were introduced to Japan during the Kamakura period by Zen monks.

sumi: charcoal sawn into various lengths and laid in the fire in a prescribed manner.

sumi-demae: the procedure for adding charcoal to the fire performed in front of the guests. The host performs this procedure either once or twice during a tea gathering depending on its duration.

tana: light wooden stand for resting or displaying certain utensils during a tea ceremony.

tatami: floor covering in the form of blocks padded with straw and covered in rush matting. Tatami come in set sizes and act as a unit of measurement in traditional Japanese architecture

teishu: the host of a tea gathering.

temae: general term for the ritual preparation of tea, or specifically the procedure used in the serving of tea or changing the fire.

tenmoku: a tea bowl with a narrow foot and broad rim originally produced in Fukien Province in China and highly prized by Japanese tea masters. The name of this ware is taken from a mountain in China. Since the Edo period, these bowls have come to be used on very formal occasions when tea is offered to Shinto or Buddhist deities or to members of the nobility. It is thought that the name derives from Mt. Tenmoku, where the first priests who went to China to study discovered them.

tenmoku-dai: a special stand on which the *tenmoku* tea bowl is placed, also introduced to Japan from China. Shaped like a saucer with a small bowl on top and a high foot, it is usually made of plain or lacquered wood.

tenugui: a rectangular cotton hand towel used to dry the hands and mouth after rinsing them with water at the stone washbasin before entering the tea room.

tobi-ishi: stepping stones in the inner tea garden.

toko: also *tokonoma*. The alcove in a tea room or a drawing room. It can either be decorated with a scroll of calligraphy or a painting, a vase of flowers, an incense container, or some combination of these. The structure of the alcove varies according to the overall design of the room or house.

tsukubai: stone washbasin. Guests crouch on a flat stone in front of the basin to wash their hands and mouths before entering the tea room.

tsume: the last guest. See "kyaku."

usucha: literally "thin tea." About two scoops of powdered tea are whisked with two-thirds of a ladle of hot water. The tea is the same high-quality powdered tea as used in *koicha* (thick tea), but less is used.

yobanashi: a tea ceremony held from the early evening to late at night during the cold season when the fire pit is used.

yoritsuki: a room in the main house where guests first gather to prepare for the tea gathering and wait for the other guests to arrive. It is sometimes a separate building in the outer garden.

yūzari: a tea ceremony held from the early evening to late at night during the warm months when the portable brazier is in use.

zen: tray traditionally used in formal dinner parties for serving a meal to guests.

Index

（新装版）茶の心
The Tea Ceremony / TP

2000 年 1 月　第 1 刷発行
2009 年 5 月　第 6 刷発行

著　者　　大日本茶道学会

発行者　　富田 充

発行所　　講談社インターナショナル株式会社
　　　　　〒112-8652　東京都文京区音羽 1-17-14
　　　　　電話　03-3944-6493（編集部）
　　　　　　　　03-3944-6492（営業部・業務部）
　　　　　ホームページ　www.kodansha-intl.com

印刷・製本所　　共同印刷株式会社